Philosophy and practical education

Philosophy and practical education

John Wilson
Department of Educational Studies
University of Oxford

Routledge & Kegan Paul
London, Henley and Boston

First published in 1977
by Routledge & Kegan Paul Ltd
39 Store Street,
London WC1E 7DD,
Broadway House,
Newtown Road,
Henley-on-Thames,
Oxon RG9 1EN and
9 Park Street,
Boston, Mass. 02108, USA
Set in IBM Press Roman by
Express Litho Service (Oxford)
and printed in Great Britain by
Lowe & Brydone Printers Ltd
Thetford, Norfolk

British Library Cataloguing in Publication Data

Wilson, John

Philosophy and practical education. –
(Students library of education).
1. Education – Philosophy
I Title II Series
370.1   LB17   77–30027

ISBN 0 7100 8675 X

The Students Library of Education has been designed to meet the needs of students of Education at Colleges of Education and at University Institutes and Departments. It will also be valuable for practising teachers and educationists. The series takes full account of the latest developments in teacher-training and of new methods and approaches in education. Separate volumes will provide authoritative and up-to-date accounts of the topics within the major fields of sociology, philosophy and history of education, educational psychology, and method. Care has been taken that specialist topics are treated lucidly and usefully for the non-specialist reader. Altogether, the Students Library of Education will provide a comprehensive introduction and guide to anyone concerned with the study of education, and with educational theory and practice.

Contents

Preface   ix

Introduction   1

1   Education   6

2   School   19

3   Discipline   33

4   Authority   48

5   Curriculum   62

6   Subjects   77

7   Autonomy   96

8   Creativity   111

Postscript   123

References   129

Preface

There are many ways of relating philosophy to education: this book attempts only one way. It arises from protracted discussions with teachers and others, and from the practical necessity of having to arrange lectures and seminars in a university department where time is short and most of the clientèle have little or no philosophical training.

Under such conditions (which apply to most contexts in which 'philosophy of education' goes on), I do not think much is gained by attempting some general coverage of topics usually thought appropriate to 'philosophy of education'; partly because it is not clear that these topics *are* appropriate, and partly because they cover far too much ground. This approach may dilute philosophical thinking to the point of tastelessness and result in potted philosophical doctrines which are regurgitated in examinations, thus boring both examinees and examiners. Nor is anything gained, other than a deceptive appearance of trendiness, by a prolonged consideration of contemporary 'ideologies' or 'movements' or fashionable educational sages. Finally, whilst it is important (for both pedagogical and philosophical reasons) that philosophers of education should have had wide experience in practical education, it does not help teachers if discussion gets bogged down at the level of very specific, day-to-day practical problems; they have to understand how such problems lead us, pretty quickly and directly, to conceptual points. Unless they can both get the taste, and see the relevance, of tough-minded conceptual argument, 'philosophy of education' will be, for them, largely a waste of time.

Accordingly I have selected a number of topics of which I take it to be true that (1) they are necessarily of direct practical concern to teachers and other educators; (2) an increase in our conceptual clarity suggests, fairly unambiguously, certain kinds of practical action; (3) they have not been properly dealt with in existing philosophical literature. I owe a debt to past and present student-teachers and others for help and advice in making this selection; and another debt to the work of Professor Peters, Professor Hirst and others, who have succeeded in making something serious and respectable out of 'philosophy of education'. That I shall refer to some of this work frequently and critically should be taken to indicate that we now have something worth criticizing; any conscientious author in this field must stand on their shoulders, however heavily.

It seems to me necessary, or at least pedagogically useful, to make some fairly strong and obvious connections with this work. A possible criticism of the present state of the subject is not only that, as Peters says, 'philosophy of education is, at the moment, suffering from too little fundamental divergence in points of view' (Peters, 1973, p. 4) — that, indeed, might inspire yet more giant theses about 'the aims of education', something we can well do without: it is also, and I think more importantly, that it suffers both in style and content (if indeed these are separable in philosophy) from a lack of dialectic. I make no apology, therefore, for some quotation and detailed criticism of passages from the current literature. To leave it entirely on one side would be not only improper but also unrealistic, since it continues to exercise a considerable influence in most of the relevant institutions.

Finally I must express my particular gratitude to Richard Peters for many helpful suggestions; and also to Celia Dusoir for many hours of fruitful philosophical discussion.

JBW
Oxford, 1976

Introduction

In the Preface I promised that the topics covered in this book would be 'of direct practical concern to teachers', and played safe by adding 'and other educators': thereby embracing local authorities, 'curriculum developers', and even perhaps professors of education. In one way, such a wide promise is easy to keep: almost anything 'to do with education' is or may be 'of direct practical concern' to teachers and others – particularly if they can find the time and energy to stand back from their daily work, read books, reflect about 'aims' and so forth. But obviously in another way this is a cheat; and we would naturally distinguish between things which almost any teacher *has* to be concerned about in a 'direct' and 'practical' way, such as maintaining discipline and teaching his subject(s), and things which he may (perhaps ought) to be concerned about, but which are not necessarily his immediate responsibility, such as the curriculum, or setting and streaming, or whether there is any sensible educational aim marked by 'autonomy'.

The trouble with this distinction, however, is that it seems to depend almost entirely upon contingent and very changeable social facts. Thus one could think of schools in which someone else (not the classroom teacher) in effect copes with the maintenance of discipline, or in which a lot of the subject-teaching or information-giving is done by teaching machines or closed-circuit television; or conversely, schools in which teachers are made collectively responsible for the curriculum, grouping in the school, and the choice of educational aims. So even for practical (let alone conceptual) purposes, in a changing world, this distinction is too fragile; and clearly we may not get much further by conducting a 'linguistic analysis' of the *word* 'teacher' – that may tell us nothing interesting. So how can we proceed?

In practice, of course, it is important for a particular teacher in a particular school to know what he *has* to do (i.e. in order to avoid getting the sack, making his own life a misery, etc.) as against what *could* be helpful to him. It may also be useful to look at what other

1

teachers, in different societies or different conditions from himself, are actually concerned with. But we are surely led inevitably to some such questions as 'What *ought* teachers to regard as "of direct practical concern" to themselves?'; and by 'ought' here we must *not* imply only that it would be nice if teachers added certain tasks to those tasks they *had* to perform. Too many books and institutions of teacher-education take it for granted that teachers have to engage in certain tasks (which are, goodness knows, demanding enough already) and then proceed to load them down with other tasks which they are made to feel they 'ought' to undertake — learning more about philosophy, psychology and sociology, discussing 'the aims of education', 'curricular theory', and a thousand and one other things. We have somehow to step back from or get behind this picture.

Suppose, as I shall argue, that there are certain things which ought to go on in schools and which are very important. These things might not be things which teachers *have* to do, in the sense that if they do not do them they get the sack; but equally they might not be just things which it would be *nice if* teachers could somehow manage to add to their tasks — they might be much too important for that, indeed they might be more important than what teachers *have* to do. To take a parallel, if I wish to stress the importance of love (and whatever activities and arrangements might generate or reinforce love) in marriage, I shall not want to say either that there *has* to be love in marriage, in the sense that marriage is contractually impossible without it, or that 'ideally' it is desirable to have love. I shall want to say that love may be more important than the contractual or 'practical' aspects of marriage, and certainly more important than any 'nice' trimmings or top-dressings (as perhaps having a nice house or long holidays together); I shall want to represent it not as an ideal but as some kind of *necessity*.

But *what* kind of necessity? There is another danger to avoid here, the danger of building up one's own preferences (values, prejudices, fantasies, etc.) into some 'theory of education' which one then claims as 'necessary'. Thus for some people it appears 'necessary' that schools should be 'progressive', and give children as much 'freedom' as possible; to others, that there should be 'standards', 'discipline', 'serious study', 'a Christian atmosphere', and so on. These are the debates that go on all the time, and very boring they are too. On the other hand, it will not help to attempt any formulation of conceptual or logical necessity, at least if this is too simple or superficial. Thus we could, of course, show that certain things followed from the meanings of such words as 'teacher' and perhaps 'school' or 'education'; but then it would always be possible for someone to make the move of saying 'All right, then, let's not have teachers but "child helpers": not schools but "convivial institutions" ', or whatever linguistic change would fit his preferred picture.

Nevertheless, there are certain permanently valid truths to which one can point. One might say, very roughly, that these truths lie not so much *in* the use of various words as *behind* it, so that they are not easily escaped simply by using different words. Thus I shall try to show, in chapter 2, that there is a certain *concept* (whether or not we are going to mark it by the word 'school') that any serious educator must work with; or again, in chapter 3, that there are certain *principles* (whether or not marked by 'discipline') which are logically necessary for all or most human enterprises. We are not, then, only or even chiefly concerned with 'the meaning of words', we are concerned rather to elicit *from* words those concepts and principles which are, as I shall try to show, permanent and necessary features of serious education.

The word 'serious' is worth stressing, because this procedure both requires some seriousness in the first place, and is intended to make us more serious. The seriousness required consists essentially of the recognition that we are, in fact, in a great deal of confusion about these concepts and principles, and a sincere desire to get clearer. We become more serious by pursuing that desire: getting clearer frees us from the pressures of prejudice, fantasy, fashion, inertia and the unconscious corruption of institutional arrangements which we take for granted. These are the chief enemies both of philosophy and of effective education. For I maintain (see Wilson, 1975) that education suffers, not so much from lack of money or effort or enough 'research-findings' produced by psychologists and social scientists, but rather from the lack of seriousness. We need clarity, common sense, and a refusal to tolerate nonsense or be bullied by contemporary climates of opinion.

If a person pursues the ideas of common sense and clarity far enough, he inevitably ends up by doing philosophy. Too many people, including (I fear) some teachers, still see 'philosophy' as something rather remote, high-minded, grand, 'abstract', and irrelevant to practical concerns. The opposite is true; nearly always, in disputes about educational practice, the *most* 'practical' thing a teacher can do is to sit down and think hard — or, better, argue with other people — about what is *meant by* the terms that crop up in such disputes. (There are hundreds of such terms: 'education', 'integration', 'examination', 'comprehensive', 'mixed ability', 'discipline', 'creativity' and so on. In this book I have had to confine myself to a few that seem of particular importance.) As he does this, he becomes much more critical of the vagueness or nonsense that is so often apparent in what is said and written (even by well-known and highly-placed 'authorities'); and he comes to get a firmer grasp of the basic truths and principles that should govern our thought and action in education.

In the following chapters I shall try to make some of these truths clearer; and in so far as I am successful, it should also become clear just how far, and how disastrously, these truths have been forgotten.

3

What is basically wrong (as I see it) with practical education, in this country and other similar societies, results from this forgetfulness. Instead of retaining a firm grasp of the logic of these truths, we waste our time in pointless conflicts between 'progressive' and 'traditional', 'child-centred' and 'authoritarian', 'left-wing' and 'right-wing' prejudices. It is as if scientific matters were at the mercy of different gangs of alchemists and astrologers, or as if medicine were left to decisions made by conflicting parties of witch-doctors and faith-healers. The façade of academic respectability and institutionalized scholarship which the subject of education now has in our society is, for the most part, nothing but a façade: it masks our confusion and ignorance.

This needs to be said, because the only way out is for those actively engaged in the business — and that means, chiefly, practising teachers — to fight their own way towards clarity. Our present confusion is not, or certainly not only, the fault of teachers: it is the fault of educationalists and politicians who pretend to knowledge and certainty, and foist such pretences on to those who actually confront our children. In so far as teachers are to blame, it is for being so deferential, or humble, or anxious, as to accept this situation and play along with it; though even this is excusable, since teachers have very little power over their own jobs (when compared with other professions) and are, in effect, constrained to accept much of the pressures of fashion and politics that are put upon them. Nevertheless, it is only by abandoning such deference — without going to the extreme of inventing one's own ideology or 'educational theory', or joining some sectarian gang — that we can even begin the long haul back to seriousness.

What, then are these basic concepts or ideas which teachers and other educators need to be clear about? The first and most obvious involves the whole nature of the enterprise in which they are engaged, an enterprise for which 'education' is (at least *prima facie*) a fair marker. Just what *is* it to 'educate' somebody? What sort of benefits or 'goods' is education concerned to produce? This will be our concern in chapter 1. In chapter 2, under the heading of 'School', we shall look at what sort of institution, with what powers, is required for this enterprise: and the following chapters, 3 'Discipline' and 4 'Authority', are about what we might (rather grandly) call the necessary political or social requirements connected with obedience, rules and contracts. In chapters 5 and 6 we turn our attention to the content of education, and try to make some sense of the extremely difficult problems involved in the ideas of a 'curriculum' and of different school 'subjects'. Finally in chapters 7 and 8 we shall be concerned with two (much-canvassed) examples of more general objectives, which might be called 'powers of the mind', under the headings of 'autonomy'and 'creativity'.

The truths which (I hope) will emerge from the discussion can, I think, be fairly seen as hanging together and forming a distinct 'thesis'.

This should become clearer when we consider the enterprise of education in chapter 1; and I have added a postscript at the end of the book
which may help to co-ordinate the points we have made. But I should
not like the reader to approach the book as one who is going to end by
agreeing or disagreeing with a 'thesis': any weight it may have lies not
in a set of 'answers' or 'conclusions', but in helping the reader to
ground his own beliefs on a basis of improved logic and clarity. If
philosophy has 'conclusions', they are not worth much by themselves;
the working is almost everything. I shall be more than content if I can
shed some new light: particularly if, in so doing, I can persuade the
practical educator that the distinctions and problems are — as one
teacher put it to me — 'not just philosophical but real'.

Chapter one

Education

A very great deal has been written under headings like 'the aims of education', 'the nature of education', 'the concept of education' and so forth, most of which is (in my judgment) more confusing than helpful. It is better to start by asking ourselves what it is that we are trying to get clear *about* by such discussions: why we *need* to consider the 'concept' or the 'nature' of education. Suppose we are teachers, or educational administrators, or researchers, or civil servants in some ministry of education: what is the *point* of engaging in philosophical reflection about education?

To this, I think, the answer is reasonably clear. It is, quite simply, so that we have an adequate and consciously-held view about what we are trying to do, about the nature of the enterprise in which we are engaging. Now of course actual people in actual jobs — teachers, civil servants, and so on — will be engaged from time to time in many different enterprises. A teacher does not only teach: he may keep the register, referee football matches, attend union meetings, and so on — and in time of war, or some other crisis, he may find himself having to keep his pupils safe from bombs or plague. Similarly a doctor does not only cure people: he may also have to fill in forms, keep accounts, tidy his consulting-room, and all sorts of other things. But we (rightly) have the feeling that there is some enterprise with which these people are, or ought to be, specially connected: something which is *central* to what they do. Just as doctors are centrally concerned with medicine and promoting health, so — we may feel — teachers and others are, or ought to be, centrally engaged in the enterprise of *educating*. Education is, so to speak, what teachers are *for* (cf. Hirst and Peters, 1970, pp. 17—19).

This feeling, so far vaguely expressed, does not allow us to conclude that the other enterprises are unimportant, or ought somehow to be got rid of. Much will plainly depend on circumstances. If we are attacked by barbarians or have not enough to eat, it will no doubt be sensible for teachers (and perhaps even doctors) to stop teaching (curing) and turn their attention to getting food for themselves and other people, or to fending off enemy attacks. The feeling is rather that there are *in principle* — 'in theory' if you like, though we hope also in practice — enterprises whose nature just *is* different. Educating people is one thing, curing them is another, keeping them properly fed is yet another, and so on. We have different words which may fairly mark these enterprises — 'education', 'medicine', 'economics'; but the words in themselves may not give us a sufficient grasp of what the enterprises are and how they differ from each other. For the enterprises exist in their own right ('in principle' or 'in theory'), whether or not people mark them clearly with certain words. Even if people did not mark them at all, or practise them at all, they would still be important: the enterprises we mark by 'science', 'medicine', 'democracy' and so on are important in themselves, even though many societies may have had no understanding of them, and lived by superstition, witch-doctoring, and tyranny.

Nevertheless one has to begin by using *some* word or words with which to conduct the discussion; and I shall start with a brief criticism of what one or two philosophers have said about 'education' — not simply for the sake of criticizing, but because it is very important to be properly aware of a number of temptations which beset us here. The word seems to open the door for almost any kind of partisan prejudice or fantasy; and not a few writers seem to want to keep the door open in this way. Thus when Max Black says that ' "Education" is, and should be, a term as comprehensive as "life" or "experience" ' (in Lucas, 1969, p. 283), and tells us on the next page that 'In practice, philosophy of education becomes nothing less than philosophy, without qualification or restriction' (p. 284), we recognize that things have got out of control. We know perfectly well that 'education' is *not* as 'comprehensive' a term as that; and we know that, if somebody claimed to be doing 'philosophy of education' when conducting a detailed examination of (say) Berkeley's theory of perception or Aristotle's categories, we should not readily understand him.

There are two, perhaps three, general temptations which need especial notice. The first is evident in Frankena's remark that 'Education is the process by which society makes of its members what it is desirable that they should become, either in general or in so far as this may be carried on by what are called "schools" ' (p. 288), or in O'Connor's 'The word refers to the sort of training that goes on in schools and universities and so on' (O'Connor, 1957, p. 5). Here 'education' is identified (roughly) with what we may call the educational *system* or 'what society does'. One obvious objection is that 'society' can make its members richer, or better-fed, or plenty of other 'desirable' things without doing anything to them which we should dream of describing as *educating* them; but the real danger lies in *identifying* an enterprise which exists in its own right with particular social practices or institutions.

A parallel may help here. Human beings may engage in an activity or enterprise which we may want to call 'religion' – though no doubt we are not entirely clear just what this enterprise is. It would obviously be wrong to think that this was the same as saying that there were certain people and social practices – parsons, funerals, churches, grand inquisitors, and so on – actually in existence: or even the same as saying that there were certain sets of beliefs and doctrines which were called 'religions'. For we could always ask 'Are these people (institutions, beliefs, etc.), whatever they may be *called*, actually concerned with *religion*?' and we may often find that they were not. If we identify religion with social practices, we make the same mistake as the man who is humorously quoted as saying 'When I say religion of course I mean the Christian religion, and when I say the Christian religion I mean the Church of England.' The point is not just that the man is prejudiced: it is that he has no idea of religion as an enterprise in its own right (Wilson, 1971, Part 1).

So with the notion of educating people. We may *call* certain things 'schools' and certain people 'teachers', and we may *say* that what we are doing is to educate children. But we have to be able to show that this is, in fact, what we *are* doing. The mere existence of social practices with the word 'education' attached to them shows nothing; any more than, in the police state of Orwell's *1984*, the existence of an institution called 'The Ministry of Truth' showed that the institution was, in fact, concerned with truth (rather than, as Orwell represents it, with propaganda). It is, in fact, a very open question how much that is actually education does go on in those institutions which we currently classify under that heading. Clearly we cannot answer the question until we know, or decide, what 'education' is to mark: but equally we cannot assume that the answer is given by existing institutions.

The second temptation is to use (or abuse) 'education' to endorse, not a particular set of social practices, but some particular ideal or set of values which we happen to favour. Most writers on the subject have some general ideology, or 'doctrine of man', or political or moral theory which they want to sell: and their 'educational theory' (together with what they want 'education' to mean) exists chiefly as a kind of spin-off, so to speak, from this general ideal. Thus Plato (*Laws*, 643–4, Saunders, 1970, p. 73):

When we abuse or commend the upbringing of individual people and say that one of us is educated and the other uneducated, we sometimes use this latter term of men who have in fact had a thorough education – one directed towards petty trade or the merchant-shipping business, or something like that. But I take it that for the purpose of the present discussion we are not going to treat this sort of thing as 'education'; what we have in mind is education from childhood in *virtue*, a training which produces a keen desire to become a perfect citizen who knows how to rule and be ruled as justice demands. I suppose we should want to mark off this sort of training from others and reserve the title 'education' for it alone.

A very large part of Plato's 'educational theory', in the *Republic* and elsewhere, is devoted to this particular goal: that is, to turning out 'perfect citizens' in the interests of a well-ordered state.

It is worth noticing here that it is not just the English word 'education' which tempts us in one or the other of these two directions. Other words in other languages suffer the same fate: thus Plato, in the passage above, monopolizes the Greek word *paideia* (here translated 'education') for his particular purposes, and the same can be, and has been, done with the French *l'éducation*, the German *Bildung*, and so forth. The same temptations beset words (in any language) which may mark enterprises of a fairly general nature, about which we have not taken the trouble to get clear: 'religion', 'politics', 'morals' and many others. They lure us to endorse either some existing social practices, or else our own partisan views (and, indeed, these two may obviously be more connected with each other than I have here made them appear).

A third approach is to use 'linguistic' or 'conceptual analysis'; and I hope to make clear how far this can be construed as a 'temptation', as against a perfectly proper procedure. One obvious difficulty is that it seems somewhat arbitrary to select a particular word in a particular language, used by a certain group of speakers at a certain time. Why should 'education', as used by certain twentieth-century English-speakers, be of more interest than, say, *paideia* as used by certain Greek-speakers in Athens of the classical period? The difficulty can partly be met by what we said earlier about distinguishing different enterprises, rather than being concerned just with the words that may mark them. As Hirst and Peters put it (1970, p. 8): 'the point of doing conceptual analysis, which is to get clearer about the types of distinction that words have been developed to designate. The point is to see *through* the words, to get a better grasp of the similarities and differences that it is possible to pick out.' But we have to assume that the words, which are our inevitable starting-points, have in fact developed in such a way as to designate or pick out the really important distinctions. Often this assumption is justified: there are many concepts which are, so to speak, both transcultural and inevitable — that is, which men in almost any culture are virtually bound to possess, and hence to mark by *some* words. But it remains an assumption. What the philosopher has to do is to elicit the important distinctions: how far these are to be found in actual linguistic usage cannot be determined in advance, and is ultimately a separate question.

9

In any case, if we start by engaging in this sort of analysis we have to beware that we do not fall victim to either of the two temptations mentioned earlier. If the procedure has merit, it must be partly by way of *preventing* ourselves from smuggling in our own particular values or doctrines. Thus in Peters's earlier work (1966, p. 30) he claims that 'we would not *say* that the ancient Spartans had received a military or moral education' and similarly, having said some fairly stringent things about the necessity for 'commitment', 'being on the inside of' various intellectual activities, and 'a man's outlook' being 'transformed by what he knows', he adds (p. 31): 'I do not think that we would *call* a person "educated" whose knowledge was purely external and inert in this way [i.e. who did not possess these attributes].' These are overt linguistic claims, and very dubious ones. Similarly (in Tibble, 1966, p. 71): ' "Education" . . . encapsulates criteria to which a family of processes must conform. The first is that something valuable should be transmitted in a morally unobjectionable manner'; but one might have strong moral objections to, say, very severe methods of teaching Latin grammar and plenty of other things, and yet think that one had (*pro tanto*) been educated or even well educated by so learning them.

In his later writings Peters makes it clear that his concern is with a 'more recent and specific concept' of education, a concept which implies 'the development of states of a person that involve knowledge and understanding in depth and breadth', and which also implies that these states are desirable (Hirst and Peters, 1970, p. 25). This is, by and large, the concept explicated by Hirst and Peters conjointly, and they recognize that it is only *one* concept that 'education' might mark: 'in so far as we are concerned about education in what we called its specific sense, we are committed to processes which assist the development of desirable states in a person involving knowledge and understanding' (p. 40). Other writers (Downie, 1974, p. 173) similarly stipulate a particular meaning for 'education', derived from some (very sophisticated) notion of 'the educated man' (ibid., pp. 11ff.).

However much interest there may be in outlining — one might fairly say, creating or fashioning — these 'specific' concepts of education, or in simply stipulating what 'education' is to mean, it is entirely plain that we are no longer engaged in conducting a non-partisan analysis of how words are used. We are being asked to direct our attention to a particular concept which the (various) authors think to be very important; as Hirst and Peters (1970, p. 41) put it, they 'are conscious that a definite moral point of view is implicit in their approach', and disappoint us by adding 'but it is not part of the intention of this book to attempt any explicit justification of it'. But our attention will only be engaged if this particular concept *is shown* to be important. We want to know whether it is, and why it is, and what sort of importance it has ('moral' importance is only one kind of importance). If this is not done, all that we have is just another attempt to promote a particular idea or set of values, this time put together in a rather confusing way with the quite different business of 'conceptual analysis'.

So far as I can see, these and other similar manoeuvres are not only mistaken but largely unnecessary. As I have suggested elsewhere (Wilson, 1975, chapter 1), there is a concept which, when properly explicated, makes tolerably clear the kind of enterprise we need to distinguish, and — though this is, in one way, a secondary consideration — best fits the term 'educate' as now normally used by English-speakers (and, I would add, other parallel terms that exist in other languages). To state this as briefly as possible: 'education' is the marker for a particular enterprise or activity, which has as its aim or 'good' the sustained and serious learning of rational creatures, planned in some coherent or overall way. We educate people (rather than treating them in other ways) when we are engaged in bringing such learning about; and people become educated — using that term as the ordinary past participle passive of 'educate', and not with any ideological accretions — when or in so far as they have done some learning of this kind. (A good parallel can be found in the Latin 'doctus', which can either mean just 'having been taught' ['having learned'], or something much more specific like 'cultured', 'well-read', 'learned'.)

Compared with the particular pictures presented by most authors, this is a fairly broad concept; but it is, I think, the concept that most contemporary English-speakers do actually mark by such terms. There is some delimitation on what learning will count as education: we do not use the term of trivial or fragmentary bits of learning, nor of the learning of animals or infants. But we do use it where what is learned may be undesirable (bad habits, or to hate Jews, or plenty of other things): and where the amount of knowledge or understanding is very small (one can learn, in a serious and sustained way, to acquire certain habits or skills or attitudes). We speak of *bad* — that is, not just incompetent but evil — education (just as we can speak of bad religion, bad moral principles, bad political ideals, and so on: we have to distinguish these from cases which are not cases of religion, or morality, or politics at all); and also of education that does not involve much knowledge or understanding.

This (very brief) sketch needs to be supplemented by two elaborations. First, some delimitation, not so much of content as of general intention, is placed on the concept of education by virtue of the fact that education is a rather general or comprehensive kind of enterprise. Thus the *Oxford English Dictionary* speaks of 'systematic instruction, schooling or training', and for 'educate' gives 'to bring up (young persons) from childhood so as to form (their) habits, manners, intellectual and physical aptitudes'. Not just any learning counts as education; the learning has to be seen as part of a systematic and coherent enterprise. Hence the grammar of 'educate' is different from the grammar of (for instance) 'train'; we can train people in particular skills, or for particular tasks, or as fillers of particular roles. But we can only educate people as such: that is, if we claim to educate people, we claim to be viewing their learning from some general, overall or comprehensive point of view, not just with an eye on certain jobs or skills.

Of course since people have minds, and education consists of learning, it is likely that a large part of this enterprise will be seen as developing knowledge and understanding in people; indeed, an educational ideal which involved *no* such development would be hard to conceive. Yet one might easily think that the really important things for people to learn − still in a comprehensive and coherent sort of way − did not involve much intellectual or 'cognitive' sophistication, but were more in the area marked by 'character', 'habits', 'attitudes' and so forth; and one might believe that these things were best learned by imitation, or practice, or exhortation, or playing games, or other methods of that kind. Again, one might think it rash to lay down any particular content as being 'really important' for *all* pupils − such content might reasonably vary according to the pupil's particular needs, abilities, or station in life. But the notion of education is neutral with regard to any questions of content, so long as there is an enterprise of this general kind, the title of education cannot be denied.

Second, some delimitation arises from the fact that 'education' normally marks a fairly formal, structured or institutionalized enterprise: something designed to raise people above the level of what they would naturally learn for themselves in the ordinary course of events. We do not speak of parents and other language-users educating their children, or even teaching them to talk, if the children just pick up the use of language from the adults − even though this learning might be thought crucially important for any mental development. We may, indeed, loosely say that certain people, or experiences, exercise an 'educational' effect; but 'education' and 'educate' is a much narrower term than 'bring up', 'rear', or 'nurture'.

These, I think, are at least some of the features which would emerge from a thorough and systematic study of how the words are actually used. Much more work, in my judgment, needs to be done in this field, both on English words and those terms which are, at least *prima facie*, parallel in other natural languages. But whatever may or may not be true of English and other usage, the important point is that there exists a particular kind of enterprise which needs to be delimited in this way, because it is concerned with a certain kind of 'good' − namely, learning. There are, of course, still wider concepts: 'upbringing', say, or 'what we do for children', would include a number of very different goods − at one time we are concerned with our children's health, at another with their appearance, and so on. Learning, though a broad enough idea, represents only *one* kind of interest, nor is this interest confined to children. A variety of other terms normally go along with this particular interest; we would not refer to children as *pupils,* for instance, nor to adults as *teachers,* unless we had this interest in mind.

There are, as we have already noted, other enterprises concerned with other specific goods: and it is important to see that each of these is delimited or bounded in the same sort of way. Often this is clear to us: we know pretty well when we do something to a person for *medical* reasons, and can distinguish these from *educational* or (say) *economic* reasons. A sick man may have to retire from attending the university or from his business: this may be good for his health, but bad for his education or his pocket. Sometimes, partly because of a lack of clarity about the terms and concepts in question, we are less clear. But whatever we choose to label as 'politics', or 'morals', or – to take a currently fashionable term – 'ideology', we must, if these terms are to have any clear meaning, be able to distinguish a *political* (moral, ideological) reason for doing something from another kind of reason, which means that we must be able to distinguish it from an educational reason.

In fact, if we resist the temptation to extend terms like 'political' ('moral', 'ideological', etc.) to cover more or less *any* consideration, we can already do this in many cases. It is politically desirable that, when attacked by barbarians, we should not worry too much about learning things but devote our attention to keeping our society safe. It is morally desirable that, if Romans are in danger of being burned alive, we should at least put off learning the violin until we have done what we can to help them. It is, or may be, 'ideologically' desirable (though I am not clear what 'ideologically' could sensibly mean) that children from different social backgrounds should belong to the same school or the same housing estate; but whether this improves those children's *learning* is another matter.

It is for these reasons that the concept of education, as I have tried to delimit it, cannot sensibly be seen as 'contestable', or 'dependent on one's ultimate values', or anything of that kind, any more than the concept of medicine, with its connected good of health. Indeed, we can go somewhat further than this. The enterprise of education is plainly necessary for any human society or individual, a point largely masked by those authors who prefer to adopt a much more stringent and value-impregnated concept, and then have to try to 'justify' it. The reason is that we could not come to resemble anything much like human beings, or rational creatures, unless we had done a good deal of serious and sustained learning, and it is implausible to suppose that such learning could be successfully done if it were left entirely to chance and nature. Some general or overall attempt, on a more or less wide front, to advance children's learning – whatever we may think it important to learn – seems essential if only because natural ability and circumstances are unreliable. In much the same way, some enterprise devoted to keeping people fit and healthy (that is, medicine) will be an inevitable feature of almost any society, even if different societies were to vary in their ideas of what counts as fitness or health, as they certainly vary in their ideas of how to achieve it.

Whether or not this sort of delimitation is acceptable as a 'definition of education' does not ultimately matter all that much – so long as we are clear about, and agreed on, what verbal markers we are attaching to what enterprises. Few people will deny the importance of sustained and serious learning, even though they might dispute the delimitation, and even though they might disagree about what ought to be learned (see pp. 20ff.). But we are not always as clear as we should be about the logical or conceptual requirements which the notion of sustained and serious learning itself imposes on us, and which we have to attend to if our educational practice is to prosper. There is a real danger that, under pressure from other, non-educational sources, teachers and educators may lose their grip on what must, at least, surely be regarded as central to the notion of education.

To illustrate this fully would take more than one book; but I will try to show how some of these logical implications are relevant to practice, and how they may be overlooked, by some brief illustrations:

1 The concept of learning implies at least that the learner comes to acquire some knowledge, or understanding, or increased control over the world *by paying relevant attention* to it, not just by any process. Learning is distinct from whatever we might plausibly mean by 'growth', 'development', 'conditioning' and other ways of just coming to be able, or finding oneself able, to do something. Where learning something involves conceptual or propositional understanding – and in human learning there are few, if any, cases where it does not – the attention must be 'relevant' in the sense that the learner must have reached his knowledge or understanding as a result of good reasons or proper evidence. If I misguidedly believe in astrology, and by casting horoscopes come to think that Flossie will make me a good wife, then – even if it is true that she will make me a good wife – we should hesitate to say that I had *learned* this truth. Those who are interested in learning, then, as opposed to certain kinds of end-products – bits of overt behaviour, or the trotting out of right answers – are necessarily concerned with *how* and *why* pupils behave in a certain way or believe certain things. If we are to be satisfied that they have *learned*, they will need to 'show the working', as the mathematicians say.

2 To learn a particular X – and we shall have to agree, if only provisionally, on some Xs if we are to educate at all – is to make

progress, by paying relevant attention, towards the understanding or mastery of X. The vast bulk of Xs have a distinct *structure*, loosely hierarchical in that there will always be some things which the learner needs to have a grasp of before he can go on to other things. A man must be able to add before he can learn to multiply, be able to play simple notes on the piano before playing a Mozart sonata, and so forth. Any *group* of pupils learning X can only function as a group if its members have roughly similar attainments in the subject. For what is actually learned at any one time will be a particular staging-post, as it were, *en route* to X: first the numerical digits, then addition, then multiplication, and so on. If the group are supposed to be learning to multiply, then nobody can be a member of it if he does not know already how to add (nor, of course, if he already knows how to multiply). This applies, *mutatis mutandis*, to all or almost all Xs and sets fairly severe logical limits on practical arrangements for group-learning.

3 If someone is a serious learner of X — that is, seriously wants to understand or master X — then it is a point of logic that he will want to find out how well he is doing, what his progress has been, what his characteristic mistakes are, how he stands in relation to other learners, and so on. *Some* application of broad notions marked by 'examination', 'assessment', 'success' and 'failure', even 'competition', is therefore a mark of serious learning. Whatever our practical applications of these ideas may be, they will clearly have to bring out (rather than mask or deny) the success or failure of various learners in their learning; for the awareness of success or failure is something to be welcomed by any serious learner. If we see dangers in this (for instance, making stupid pupils feel depressed or allowing clever ones to feel arrogant), then we must deal with them by other methods which do not interfere with serious learning, either that, or — as we may easily find ourselves doing, in an unconscious sort of way — give up or water down the idea of serious learning altogether (cf. Wilson, 1972b, Part 4).

4 Certain things, like adding a cubit to one's stature, cannot be learned and we must not deceive ourselves by putting these things in the category of *educational* objectives. But certain other things *can only* be acquired by learning. We cannot, for fairly obvious logical reasons, condition or browbeat a person into loving his neighbour, or appreciating poetry, or being keen on philosophy, or doing anything that involves appropriate perceptions and the adoption of rational attitudes. We may obtain 'brute' behaviour by other methods but for some objectives such methods are non-starters. We thus have to think hard about how much value we put on these objectives as against others: about how much time and resources, in the case of particular pupils,

we are going to spend on those aims which are, as it were, *uniquely* connected with learning (education). I do not think there is a single determinate answer to the question, if only because much will depend on the particular context and the particular pupils; but it is a question more easily answered if we are clear about what the concept of learning involves.

Current disputes under headings like 'mixed ability', 'examinations', 'setting' and 'streaming', 'going comprehensive', 'the curriculum' and many others are (it is fair to say) usually conducted without the benefit of these and similar conceptual points. I hope to have made their general relevance obvious enough: and this, indeed, is sufficient for my purposes here, because by far the most important thing is that teachers and other educators should *themselves* work out the points more fully and relate them to practical decisions. The philosopher by himself can only start this ball rolling: it is for the practical educator to pick it up, keep possession of it despite all the pressures from non-educational (or even anti-educational) sources, and take it over the goal-line.

I do not imply that conceptual points about learning are the only, or even the most important, conceptual points which relate to educational practice. As Peters puts it (1973, p. 2), philosophy of education 'draws on . . . established branches of philosophy and brings them together in ways which are relevant to educational issues'. But it is essential to keep a firm hold of the idea of serious and sustained learning in order to know just *what* conceptual points are relevant, or just what 'established branches of philosophy' we need to 'draw on'. If we do not do this, practical educators can too easily come to see 'philosophy of education' as something rather grandiose. What we have to do is to hang on to the notion of education, be clear about the nature and force of conceptual argument in general, and take it from there.

In this book, then, I am concerned only to elucidate and apply *some* of the concepts and principles which seem to relate most directly to the enterprise of education, as delimited earlier. There are, in fact, a great many of these; and I think practical educators can get quite a long way by agreeing about them, and putting them to work, before entering upon much more complicated and uncertain disputes. As I see it (though this needs much more discussion) the main areas for dispute are twofold. First, we may argue about the *amount* of concern we should have for education as against other enterprises: about how we are to weigh or measure educational goods against other goods. Since this book is primarily intended for practical educators, who are (so to speak) in the business already, I shall not be considering this question at length. Second, however, we may argue about *what*, or what sorts of, things it is important to learn; and with this we shall be, at least indirectly, concerned in the last parts of the book (chapters 5 to 8). So something needs to be said about this here.

Aristotle presents the problem when he says in the *Politics* (Book VIII, chapter 2, in Sinclair, 1962, p. 300):

> For in modern times there are opposing views about the practice of education. There is no general agreement about what the young should learn either in relation to virtue or in relation to the best life; nor is it clear whether their education ought to be directed more towards the intellect than towards the character of the soul . . . it is not certain whether training should be directed at things useful in life, or at those conducive to virtue, or at non-essentials.

If we have failed to make much advance in this problem since Aristotle, this is likely to be partly (perhaps chiefly) because we have failed to produce and elucidate an adequate set of *categories* of what sorts of things there are to learn: categories without which we should not know just *what it was* that, in each case, we were going to defend as 'an important sort of thing to learn'. Part of the difficulty is that the objects of learning are so various: one can — to speak only at the grammatical level — learn that X, or how to X, or to X, or just X. But remarks of this kind could only form a mere beginning to an enormous taxonomic task, which cannot be attempted here.

What we can do, however, is to avoid taking up our options too quickly. In particular it is important to bear in mind one distinction between different sorts of Xs that can be learned. On the one hand, there are Xs like 'Latin', 'trigonometry', 'music', 'horsemanship' and many others, which seem to be titles for what might be called subjects, or bodies of knowledge, or crafts, or sets of skills. On the other hand, one can learn patience, or to be prudent, or not to show resentment, or how to make one's wife happy, and these seem to involve (at least in some cases) something more like dispositions or virtues or mental powers. It might, perhaps, be said that the former are (as it were) the direct objects of 'learn', and the latter more indirect; and in any case the distinction is a rough one which cannot be fully worked out here. But it is very striking that, at least for many of us nowadays, the notion of education or learning is much more likely to suggest the former than the latter, though this would certainly not have been true for Plato, Aristotle, or many subsequent thinkers.

Among the reasons for this prejudice may be a feeling of uncertainty about *what* mental powers or virtues (if any) we want our pupils to learn; the idea, largely unexamined, that anyway they are not the sorts of things that can be *learned*; our peculiar attachment to the restricted notion of 'learning' whereby we see only 'the curriculum' or 'subjects' as learnable; the too-rapid willingness to turn over the whole business to psychology, to be dealt with under the heading of 'motivation' or 'attitude'; and a set of very various social conditions, which have caused us to take for granted that schools do not concern themselves with this sort of thing. Of these ideas, perhaps the most crippling is that which lies behind the first reason: the semi-conscious doubt whether making our pupils learn *anything* in this area would not be 'indoctrinatory', 'authoritarian', 'imposing our own cultural values' and so forth.

Part of my intention in this book is to show this to be a false alarm. In reference to what may be called the social or structural requirements for any serious education (chapters 2 to 4), its falseness is, I think, fairly obvious. For here certain arrangements can be seen to be conceptually necessary, and the deployment of certain concepts seen to be inevitable. There is, however, less certainty about the content of education, both in regard to 'the curriculum' and 'subjects' and in regard to the mental powers and virtues just mentioned; and this is, as I have said, chiefly because we do not have a clear set of categories to work with. What I shall say about the former (chapters 5 and 6) is chiefly designed to shed some light on this problem of categorization; and the same is true in some degree of chapters 7 and 8, in which I consider two fairly topical examples of such powers or virtues − 'autonomy' and 'creativity' − which illustrate the problem quite well.

I hope that what I have to say in these latter chapters will, at least, make one or two important things clear. First, though the content of education is largely disputable, it is not entirely so. There seem to be some 'basic skills' or competencies, such as literacy, which would be necessary or advantageous for more or less *any* serious and sustained learning; and there seem also to be some mental powers, or mental stances, of which the same is true − perhaps those that might be marked by 'seriousness', 'ego-strength', 'love of the truth' or even 'creativity' (chapter 8). Second, we shall not be clear about how much room there is for dispute, or even what a sensible dispute would look like, until we are much clearer about what we *mean by* the various markers that are held up as educational objectives or important 'things to be learned'. For until we have reached this stage, we cannot even *see just what* the 'values' or 'ideals' are that we imagine ourselves to be supporting, nor whether they can, in fact, be regarded as educational objectives − that is, things to be *learned* rather than acquired by other methods.

There is, obviously, an immense amount of work to be done in all these areas by both philosophers and practical educators. But meanwhile the latter, at least, have to get on with the job. What vitiates practical education is not, or not only, our failure as philosophers to be entirely clear about *all* the concepts and problems that are relevant; such utopias should be worked for, but not waited for. The point is rather that there are *some* things, of the utmost practical importance, about which we can be quite clear enough for practical purposes − provided we keep our heads.

Chapter two

School

In this chapter I want to point to certain elements, features or arrangements as being conceptually or logically necessary for more or less *any* seriously-held set of views about the education of children, and hence for *any* sort of 'school'. Of course this is a bold claim, the merits of which might ultimately depend on when a set of views can be said to be 'seriously held'. But it would, I think, include all or nearly all the current views about 'the aims of education', whether of the 'left' or the 'right'; and part of my aim is to cut down the constant discussions that involve this very boring 'left—right' polarization, by focusing attention on these 'necessary' elements — elements which are, in fact, very largely absent from most schools in our own and in many other societies.

As I hope to have shown in chapter 1, not just anything counts as education. There are plenty of things we can do to, or for, children besides educate them, and some of these we can do in what may still be called 'schools'. We can exercise some sort of custody over them, keep them off their parents' hands or off the job market or off the streets, ensure that they have at least one square meal a day, and enable them to mix with children of different social classes. But if a school is to educate, then those who run it must arrange that the pupils do some serious and systematic learning: the enterprise must be planned in some general or overall way, and result in learning which would not occur in the ordinary course of nature.

My claim is that certain fairly substantive conclusions follow from this, conclusions which are perhaps obvious, but which have been masked or neglected by the partisan adoption of particular educational aims and methods (together with aims and methods that may not merit the term 'educational'). Our advocacy of particular 'values', of this or that particular content for education, has blinded us to what *any* serious attempt to educate logically requires. This comes about, I think, simply by taking up partisan positions too quickly, just as definitions of education themselves may go astray because we want *our* kind of education to flourish.

To show how this happens in full detail would require much more space, but I will start by trying to show how features necessary to any kind of education can be embedded or mixed up in one particular kind of educational ideal. This ideal is clearly formulated in a coruscating and sensible article by Oakeshott (Dearden *et al.*, 1972, pp. 19ff.), about what he calls 'School'. 'School', he says, involves 'a serious and orderly initiation into an intellectual, imaginative, moral and emotional inheritance' with 'a considered curriculum of learning': 'an engagement to learn by study', which is 'a difficult undertaking' and 'exacting' (p. 24). Another 'component of the idea "School" is that of detachment from the immediate, local world of the learner. . . . "School" is "monastic" in respect of being a place apart where excellences may be heard because the din of worldly laxities and partialities is silenced or abated' (p. 25). Most of Oakeshott's article is devoted to an explication of this 'engagement', and an entertainingly destructive account of various attempts to 'abolish "School", first by corrupting it and then by suppressing it' (p. 27).

I should like to connect this with remarks made by many other able philosophers of education, even though we shall have to wrench them unfairly from their contexts. Herbst, for instance, ends by saying 'If by education we produce men and women of excellence, we have no need of a higher aim' (Peters, 1973, p. 74). Mary Warnock argues persuasively for the contention 'that quality in education entails learning about something, as they say, "in depth" ' (ibid., p. 119). Peters's whole view of education derives from his concept of an 'educated man' (one who is adequately initiated into some or all of the most important 'forms of thought'); and this is attached to particular 'values' which are not (Dearden *et al.*, 1972, p. 16):

> the mundane, instrumentally-oriented operations which the term 'education' has traditionally covered. . . . To draw attention, therefore, to the connexion between 'education' and the ideal outcome of an 'educated man', and to maintain that we ought to use words like 'training' or 'instruction' when we do not connect what we are doing with such an ideal, are aids to communication in the service of an overall ideal.

Now throughout these and other writings there float four quite different ideas, or perhaps more, which need to be disentangled:

1 That what we do in schools should not or not entirely be governed by 'instrumental' pressures (the demands of Herbst's 'consumer society') (Peters, 1973, pp. 65ff.), but should serve some (unspecified) ideals of their own.

2 As in (1) but with an ideal specified in terms of the development of understanding, reason, awareness, what Mary Warnock wants to make 'imagination' mean (ibid., pp. 112–13), perhaps Peters's notion of an 'educated man', or whatever.

3 That what we do in schools should be concerned with an 'exacting' and 'difficult undertaking', involving 'a considered curriculum', learning 'in depth', and the production of 'men and women of excellence', and that this is what 'education', properly considered, is *about*.

4 That 'education' may be about other ideals also (have other 'aims'), but that the aims in (2) and (3) have some sort of unique importance; rather as one might think that the ideals (supposedly) enshrined in a university were, at least from the strictly educational viewpoint, of more importance than those (perhaps) enshrined in a polytechnic or college of technology. (This is a weaker version of (2) and (3), and might itself take various forms.)

I do not say that these different ideas are confused in the minds of the authors (though one might be forgiven for suspecting so); but they are certainly confused in the public mind. The simple point is that one may maintain (1) without maintaining either (2), (3) or (4). That is, one may hold that schools, pupils and teachers should not be the mere tools of society or the puppets of social pressures – that there are *some* kind or kinds of educational or at least non-social ideals which schools should serve – *without* holding that these ideals wholly or even primarily involve (2) the development of understanding and reason, (3) an 'exacting' study concerned with 'depth', 'excellence', etc. One might reject even the weaker (4), which accepts the possibility of other 'non-social' ideals but downgrades those which are not 'educational' as described in (2) and (3). Of course this is boringly obvious when stated. One might believe, for instance, that schools should serve some otherworldly, religious ideal, and be kept wholly free from 'instrumental' or social pressures – but this ideal and its realization in the school might not have much to do with (2) the development of understanding and reason, or with (3) the 'exacting' engagement in 'a considered curriculum', 'learning in depth', etc. One might well deny these as centrally or specially important aims (4), or even deny them as important aims at all – though, of course, if we said that the school had *no* interest in developing learning, understanding and reason we might well be asked why we called it a 'school' rather than, say, an indoctrination centre or a club for mystics.

Naturally the brutal distinctions I have enforced between (2), (3) and (4) do not really hold up. There are ways in which they coalesce, and might in practical situations (in schools, universities, etc.) be better graded according to how stringently, and how generally, they employed the particular criterion of 'the development of understanding and reason'. (2) merely states this as a (or rather *the*) generalized ideal; (3) is as it were a stronger version of its application — the idea is that, if we are really serious about developing understanding, this will involve 'depth', 'a considered curriculum', a special interest in intellectual 'excellence', and so on; (4) retains this ideal and gives it a kind of priority, but allows others to operate. Of any institution one might in principle ask how *much* of its time and effort was spent on *this* ideal (generality), and of the time and effort that was so spent, how 'difficult' or 'exacting' ('professional' or 'scholarly'?) the task was planned to be (stringency).

It will be clear that public debates conducted in terms like 'academic', 'intellectual', 'élitist', 'standards', 'excellence', etc. float somewhere in this area. There is on the one side a desire to defend a *particular* ideal, perhaps statable as (2), (3) or (4), or some modification of these; and on the other side a nebulous feeling that none of these statements even begins to do serious justice to what substantial numbers of children in our schools actually need. It is this feeling that prompts many 'progressive' writers to identify the authors we have been looking at as defenders of a particular and partisan set of 'academic' or 'traditional' values; and it must, I think, be admitted that what these authors say is not always clear enough to escape this charge. What I am trying to do here is primarily to dissociate this particular debate, in which (2), (3) and (4) are items, from the quite different issue involved in (1) — that is, as we may perhaps call it, the *autonomy* of schools.

Let us go back now to Oakeshott's idea of 'School'. We should be able to disentangle (as he does not) the admittedly still vague notion of schools as 'detached', 'apart', specifically separated and shielded from the outside world, perhaps 'monastic', etc., from his quite different ideas about the particular scholarly or 'academic' functions or régimes in them. I am not sure just where Oakeshott stands in regard to these functions or régimes; nor does this matter. What matters is that we should see clearly at least the possibility that he might be right about the notion of detachment, and wrong about the rest (or rather, not so much wrong as partisan). I want to argue that this is much more than a possibility.

Suppose an ideal X, loosely attached to the term 'education', which represents whatever its proponent thinks desirable in the upbringing of children: 'freedom', 'creativity', 'a trained mind', 'relevant knowledge', 'cognitive perspective', 'moral awareness', or whatever. Then certain things seem to follow by conceptual necessity. First, he will wish to make social arrangements of some kind within which this ideal is realized in reference to children: that is, there will necessarily be certain times, places or contexts in which the children learn to acquire the relevant virtues, or knowledge, or whatever the ideal demands. This remains true even if, for instance, he thought children would be best educated just by being allowed to wander among the groves and fields. There would have to *be* groves and fields organized for the purpose, presumably not entirely infested by snakes or pterodactyls, and so on. This gives us a second point, connected with the first: he will wish these arrangements to be *secure*, protected from whatever social or other pressures might destroy or corrupt them. Again, the corruption may be of different kinds, depending on the ideal — it might consist of 'the values of the market-place' invading an ideal of scholarship, or property-developers spoiling the groves and fields, or wicked atheists corrupting a Christian community, or whatever. Third, there will necessarily be, at least in principle, some *people* who are in some sense 'expert' in understanding the ideal X and/or in helping to realize it, for children, within these social arrangements.

All this of course sounds very cumbersome; but I am anxious to make it clear that these points are independent of particular educational views, even extremist ones. Words like 'teacher', 'lesson', even 'school' itself, may mask this; maybe some children do not need a teacher but rather a guide, philosopher and friend: not lessons but 'learning experiences': not schools but 'social centres'. All such opinions do not affect these points, which hold good for any X. The only possible exception that I can imagine is the case in which X stands for any and every experience which the child may have in whatever social situation he may find himself. This might, I suppose, be one interpretation of the phrase 'letting him just grow up naturally': that is, not in accordance with some *ideal* picture of 'nature' as opposed to 'society', but rather by way of accepting and endorsing society or life itself — a sort of 'whatever is, is best' view.

I do not know whether anyone actually holds this view (if it is intelligible), but it is worth noting that many people act and talk as if they did. It is difficult to see what rationale could lie behind moves to 'integrate school with the real world', 'break down the ivory towers' and so on, other than the belief that 'society' or 'the real world' somehow instantiate a better ideal (or instantiate the right ideal better) than schools do. Of course, if all schools are — according to whatever criteria are being used — very bad, we may reasonably prefer that a child goes to no existing school at all rather than to any one that actually exists. But it will still be true that whatever is thought to be desirable in 'the real world', whatever ministers best to X, will have to be socially arranged. Fears about the evil effects of 'total institutions', 'Fascist-type boarding-schools' and so on are here irrelevant.

It seems to me that in so far as X is *seriously* maintained as an educational ideal (rather than just talked about as a fantasy in reaction to existing institutions), there will be the logical necessity of creating something like an *enclave* or 'detached' context within which the ideal is to be realized. The stronger and clearer the ideal, the more we shall make our arrangements specific, the more security we shall want them to have, and the more we shall hope to identify, train and (as I shall argue later) give power to the 'experts' who man the educational area. As soon as X is spelled out in any serious way, we shall be less and less content to see the children doing just anything or having just any experience. If a school or educational context allowed total randomness in this way, we should doubt whether those in charge had any clear educational ideals at all.

We must again stress, if boringly, the point that this is independent of the content of X. For instance, suppose (as perhaps with Neill's Summerhill) we thought it terribly important that children should make up their own rules rather than having rules imposed by teachers, that they should choose their own subjects to study rather than being browbeaten or unreasonably persuaded into a particular curriculum, that they should be free from the sexual repressions of their society, and so forth. It is at once clear that we need a very well-defined *enclave* for this, presumably one in which society's corrupting sexual norms do not enter, in which teachers carefully selected for the purpose would not impose, in which a lot of hard work was done (as Neill did) in helping — dare we say 'teaching'? — the children to make their own rules, etc. Indeed, in some respects at least, the more 'corrupting' any society or social 'establishment' is thought to be, the more well-defended and well-organized an *enclave* we shall need.

The points that follow from our being serious about X are logical, and not (so to speak) sociological: getting clear about the difference is crucial. For instance, the notion of an *enclave* is not intended territorially, though it will almost certainly work out as such. I mean that if, for instance, we thought it extremely desirable for our X that children should be moved every day from one social context to another (a lunatic but possible view), then we should still have to determine on these contexts and make proper arrangements for moving them — perhaps like whatever arrangements were available for mendicant friars or wandering scholars. We should still, in other words, have *institutional arrangements* — and probably much more complicated ones — even though the children were not kept permanently in one place: just as a philanderer has some (very complex) institutional arrangements to cope with his plethora of women, even though he does not go in for the specific institution of monogamic marriage. The notions that follow from the serious pursuit of any ideal X for education — some kind of defended institution with 'experts' in charge of it — are logically inexpellable.

It may seem logically possible, in certain terms, to reject this or deny its relevance to schools. We might accept the conceptual points made earlier, but maintain that they had no substantive applicability. There are perhaps two main ways of doing this. First, we could entertain ideals which were nothing like those usually subscribed to: for instance, we could construe the notion of a school on the analogy of a language school or a secretarial school, and our ideal (X) might be restricted to something like 'being able to speak French' or 'being able to type and do shorthand'. We should not concern ourselves with the child's psychological needs, or social abilities, or understanding in general, but only with small and circumscribed segments of these. 'Institutions' with 'experts' in charge would still be required to do even this job: but they would not need to be any more *powerful* than the job required — which would not be much. Second, we could grant the propriety of ideals which required more 'potency' for their realization, but maintain that this 'potency' should not be attached to *schools*. Other candidates would presumably be 'the family', 'the local community', 'social centres' or even perhaps 'the gang' or 'youth culture'. We rely on these to take care of the 'serious' ideals (of whatever kind), and use schools only to purvey certain segmented services.

But the objections to this are fairly obvious. One such objection would be most naturally put by saying that, if our interest were wholly confined to the offering of circumscribed services and skills, it could hardly count as an interest in *educating children*. This is not necessarily to tie 'education' down to the fairly specific notion of an 'educated' man, 'cognitive perspective', etc., but it makes the point that anything normally meant by 'educating a person' is not adequately explicated by this sort of circumscribed or segmented approach (as argued in chapter 1, pp. 11–12). If even this sounds too 'linguistic', we can say that the approach does not seem to *take children* (or the needs of children) *seriously*; and if somebody said that children (*qua* people, rather than just *qua* users of skills and services) did not have needs that ought to be taken seriously, I think we should be at a loss to understand what he could conceivably mean. Second, whilst it is of course arguable that 'schools' as we now understand the word are not 'the right sort of institution' to use and give power to, this turns out to be merely a linguistic point. Let S stand for whatever institution(s) we use to cater for the seriously-held educational needs and ideals that we entertain: then it follows that S will have to be sufficiently powerful to do this very difficult job properly.

We may now be able to spell out rather more fully just what is implied by the notion of a serious educational ideal. First, to pick up a point just made, there is the requirement that the enterprise be planned in some coherent and overall way. It is inherent in the grammar of 'educate' that we educate people *qua* people, not *qua* role-fillers or skill-users; and this means that, if I set out to educate a person, I have not only to take his needs seriously but to take *more* and *more varied* needs seriously than if I set out to cure, or train, or feed him. If I did

25

not at least seriously consider what ought to be done about his mental or intellectual development, moral or emotional maturity, grasp of important knowledge, general powers of understanding and so on, I should be attempting not education but something more limited. Educating people is more than training them, 'socializing' them, or giving them a handful of skills, bits of knowledge, or hobbies. This is not to deny either that the enterprise may be given very different kinds of content by different educators, or that other enterprises may be thought more important than education. The importance of a man's needs may be heavily context-dependent, and many of them may in any case not be met by learning. But any kind of education must at least take the range and complexity of a person's needs into account.

Second, we have to remember that education is to do with serious and sustained learning. This point must not be pressed too far: as we saw earlier, it is important to leave open questions about how much learning, how 'scholarly' the learning should be, how 'academic' a 'curriculum' we want, what the subject-matter ought to be, and so on. My point can be minimally made by saying that education will necessarily involve a regime in which pupils *do* things, not just (as would be more true of, say, a hospital or an indoctrination centre) have things done *to* them. The 'doing', in fact — particularly since it will entail learning — will be of a complicated kind: not just a matter of simple physical movements, like marching or even shouldering arms, but involving many different kinds of perception, understanding, awareness and so on. In particular, since education is to do with people, a lot of this doing and learning will necessarily involve the personal interaction of the pupils with each other and with those in charge. It will be appropriate to speak of 'the community', 'tradition', 'rules and discipline', 'learning to live together', 'love' and so on, in ways which would not be appropriate for other institutions. It is not, or not only, that the social context has to be properly structured and defended *in order to* educate, it is rather that initiation into such a context is a necessary *part of* education.

Third, there is a point which follows from the two points just made, and gives us one criterion for the selection of what we have called 'experts': that is, those properly to be entrusted with the promotion of the educational ideal in practice. From the number and complexity of the needs, the kinds of needs they are (that is, the needs of agents and learners, not just of recipients), and the peculiar importance of a 'community' appropriate to these, it follows that one criterion for being 'expert' is *knowing the pupils*, in some fairly intimate way. If we were talking, outside the sphere of education, about (say) the fluoridation of water, or some desideratum about which natural laws could be determined, equally applicable to all children, this would not be so. I do not, usually, have to *know* a particular person in order to know that aspirin will cure his headache, or that food will assuage his hunger, or money ameliorate his poverty. But in any area which is concerned with what may roughly be called 'psychological' needs, the case holds. If (which is doubtful) there are natural laws or even large-scale generalizations to be made here, not many have yet been determined. Such needs are not packageable, like aspirin. Of course there are other criteria. We have to talk, if vaguely, of the desirability that those in charge be benevolent, concerned for the good of the children rather than their own convenience (or the convenience of their prejudices); well-informed, and aware of whatever truths about children and their needs other experts can tell them; 'insightful', or good at understanding and communicating with children; and so on. If we specify the ideal more tightly — which I do not want to do here — other criteria may be added: for instance, *if* (only if) we think it important that they should learn PQR, the person will have to know enough of PQR to teach them, or at least to make the knowledge available. But it remains clear, I think, that those who know the children — helped, of course, by all the information, training and other assistance that we can give them — will be those who are best capable of determining what ideals, or aspects of ideals, and what methods of realizing them are most appropriate for those children. (Other things being equal, of course; but if other things are not equal, this means that we either have not found out how to get good teachers, or do not seriously want them.)

Fourth, a point about independence. Some degree of independence or autonomy follows logically from the fact that any serious educational ideal, as we have already argued, will be different from (and hence always liable to be in conflict with) the 'values', pressures, demands, etc., of society, as represented and enforced by governments or other power-groups. Some governments are not much concerned with serious and sustained learning (of whatever content our ideal specifics) at all; many more are concerned only with such learning as is of fairly practical value; none can be solely concerned with learning, since there are other quite different goods which it is the business of governments to promote. Of course enlightened governments may *delegate* the promotion of particular educational ideals which they favour, or at least *permit* such promotion. But in all cases there will have to be a class of people who are 'autonomous' in the sense that their sole concern is with the ideal, and that they have enough independent power to promote it. Taken in conjunction with our third point above — that the 'experts' should chiefly consist of those who know the pupils well — this yields quite powerful conclusions. We are saying that the business of education should, in general, be entrusted to certain experts who know the pupils *as opposed to* governments, bureaucrats, parents, 'educationalists', or other sources of pressure.

It may now be objected either that these points still yield no

27

substantive conclusions, or that they yield no clear ones. We have, as it were, a necessary but theoretical picture of a 'potent' and independent institution run by the people on the spot. But (it will be said) the cash value of this in practice will depend on various provisos which must be added. Thus of course society, which I suppose means the government, can make just demands on schools: demands arising from the economy and the need for social order — we have to earn a living, avoid total chaos, and fend off the barbarians. Of course parents must have some say, perhaps in the form of some choice of school, about what happens to their children. Of course we must have some kind of standard examination system, if only to check up on what has minimally to be learned or, if you like, some system of assessment and inspection to ensure that the schools are doing whatever their job may be properly. Of course schools will have to compete for money with other social institutions and requirements. And of course we may not feel all that much confidence in existing teachers to act as 'experts' in the way outlined above. Does all this not mean that, in practice, we shall have to compromise, and judge each case on its own merits?

The answer to this is 'certainly; but we must first be clear about what we are compromising *between*, and what *sort* of "merits" can be pointed to'. I am only saying that, *in so far as* our concern is with that area which may roughly be marked by 'educating children', these points apply. It is important to be clear about it, if only because we need to be clear about what we are sacrificing, if and when we have to sacrifice it. For instance, suppose we have the particular ideal of a community which pursues 'scholarship'. Then to hold this ideal seriously involves accepting (1) that the community will have to be 'potent' enough to ensure that the social conditions of 'scholarship' are satisfied within it; and (2) that only those who are themselves scholars, and who know personally the students or would-be scholars in that community, could conceivably make the right sort of judgments both about (1) and about other matters (for example, what sort of courses or curricula to run and how to run them). The notion that a bureaucrat or politician or parent or psychologist or anybody else would be more 'expert' than such people seems here plainly absurd — though they may have contributions to make (this is elaborated in Wilson, 1975, chapter 3).

We would more naturally say that the bureaucrats and administrators and others should *service* the proper experts to the best of their ability, making the aims and operations of the community, as defined and controlled by the experts, smoother and easier to attain: rather as, in an air force, the efforts of the administration, ground staff, armourers, etc., are devoted straightforwardly to keeping the air-crews operative. But, of course, the pressures of war might make it necessary to turn this community into a military training centre, and staff it with generals; or the pressures of starvation, into an agricultural commune.

More probably — and this is where clarity becomes critically important — some of its time and effort may have to be spent on pursuing other goods besides 'scholarship'.

Lack of clarity here produces interstices into which bureaucratic, political and other social pressures easily creep. The procedure we require is one by which a clear decentralization of power is subject only to highly specific demands. What we need to hear from the representatives of other than educational goods — that is, in the last resort, from governments — is something like: 'Fortunately we can afford to spend quite a lot of money on education. As politicians, we do not know much about educational ideals and practices, so we have to trust somebody and we shall trust you, the people actually running the schools on the spot, because you know the children and we have tried to select and train you as well as we know how. Spend this money as you think best for your particular children. We do, however, insist on certain things for our money: that the children you produce shall be employable; that they shall be able to read and write; that, if they want to live in this society, they understand its laws and are prepared to abide by them. You may prefer to hive off these demands from those which are made by your own educational ideals, perhaps you can cope with them all by designating one day in the week for "social requirements". Or you may prefer somehow to integrate them with whatever else you want to do with the children. But so long as you meet them, and other just demands which we shall also specify, you may do what you like the rest of the time.'

Of course this still leaves much unclear; but we may say, roughly, that it suggests a set-up much more like that of the independent schools, universities, or Oxbridge colleges than like that of most state schools in the UK — and in other countries, for the most part, the autonomy and powers of teachers in schools are much less. My claim is that the format visible in the former institutions is also necessary for the latter. Indeed, it seems plausible to say that the worse or more serious the problems we face in education (which means, I suppose, the further we descend the social scale and start thinking about really 'tough' schools with children from 'bad' homes), the more obviously necessary some such format is. One might perhaps suppose, rather after the style of a Whig aristocrat, that for 'well-bred' and socially well-placed children not very much needed to be done. They needed, perhaps, a few social accomplishments (as at a 'finishing-school') in some reasonably civilized and attractive milieu, but no very serious or *intense* education. But it is not plausible to say this of children in (for instance) Educational Priority Areas in this country: here it seems clear that, unless schools are very much more 'potent', their effect is likely to be superficial.

I have sketched out elsewhere some rough details of what I take to be necessary for a 'potent' school (Wilson, 1972b, Part 4), but these are not directly relevant. Nor need we here get involved with quasi-empirical questions about 'the professional status' of teachers, suitable types of teacher-training, etc. It will be more profitable to single out one or two very general modes of thinking which seem to inhibit these (to my mind, very obvious) moves. For it is not, I believe, the practical and administrative details which deter us: it is, rather, certain semi-conscious notions that we have not squarely examined.

The first of these we have, in effect, already observed; it might be described as the fantasy of 'guilt by association'. *Per accidens*, the idea of a potent and independent school — Oakeshott's 'School' — has been conceptually associated with specific educational ideals ('scholarship', 'academic standards', etc.) and empirically associated with schools that instantiate these (I suppose, the better public and grammar schools). It is as if people felt that they could only break the latter two links if they broke the former as well. The idea of being similar in *format*, though different in the substance of both ideal and practice, seems to many unreal or too sophisticated, even though there are innumerable state boarding schools, approved schools, schools for spastic children and so forth, which make the point very obvious.

The second is a little more subtle, and ultimately much more dangerous. It consists of the (unspoken) notion that the 'imposition' of *any* ideal on children is somehow wrong. Disenchanted, perhaps justifiably, by the unsuitability of traditional academic ideals for large numbers of what I will daringly call stupid children, many educators have reacted not by saying 'We do not want *this* ideal or *these* standards, what we want is a quite different ideal — and now we will spell this out as clearly as possible, make sure our schools are armed and powerful enough to realize it, take care that we assess and evaluate our practice to make absolutely sure that we are making progress', and so on; but in effect by saying 'since we don't want "academic" standards, we don't want standards at all'.

Usually this notion is itself clear only in the lack of any attempt at clarity about what these other ideals and standards are to be, how they are to be properly evaluated, what social and disciplinary structures in the school would help to attain them, and other relevant matters — one hears only miasmic talk about 'autonomy', 'creativity', 'child-centred education' and so forth. Occasionally attempts are made to justify particular projects or enterprises, but these are hard to take seriously because it seems that the authors themselves do not take the business of justification seriously. It is as if the whole business of justification and cognate ideas marked by such terms as 'right', 'mistake', 'standard', 'progress', 'succeed', 'fail', etc., seemed to them anathema. This feeling has some connections with the 'guilt by association' feeling mentioned a little earlier, but it goes far beyond that.

These two unite (to take a field with which I am personally very familiar) in the paradigm and seminal case of 'moral education'. We have, on the one hand, a number of individuals and institutions who wish to defend 'standards': only, they are nearly always *partisan* standards or moral views. Perhaps they insist that they be based on religion, or questionable notions of sexuality and 'decency', or certain political outlooks, or whatever: in the UK, I suppose, their representatives would be chiefly the *arrière-garde* upper and middle class, and their right-wing adherents. On the other hand, partly reacting against this line but partly in a state of profound (if unconscious) incoherence and despair about the possibility of taking any definite line at all, there are large numbers of people roughly labelled 'liberal', who would like to do something about 'moral education' but are not quite sure what: for would not *anything* have to count as an 'imposition' by 'authoritarian' teachers? Well, perhaps not everything: perhaps (the feeling is) we can be safe in just discussing with children, talking about 'controversial issues', taking our aims from them rather than ourselves,* making up all sorts of text-book material and visual aids, and so on – and this is, in fact, precisely what most practical projects in moral education have done. Nothing like a *methodology* is allowed to appear: that smacks of danger, because it smacks of rules, standards, and getting things right and wrong. So in effect, nothing deserving the name of *education* is done by either party: what we have is either a rather hopeless rearguard attempt to indoctrinate, or a general muddle.

It is in this sort of morass, I think, that most of what is called 'educational theory' is still stuck. When we keep our heads, we know perfectly well that we ought not to impose or inculcate 'standards' or behaviour-patterns in any area (not only 'moral education') on children, if these cannot be rationally defended at the bar of pure reason but appear merely as the preferences of ourselves or our society; but also that in order to educate or minister to the needs of children at all, we have to present them with and inculcate very clearly-defined standards, properly enforced and adequately institutionalized. Incidentally, this is why psychology and the social sciences have at present little that is helpful to tell us; for empirical facts are only relevant here in so far as they are related to the standards or norms which, as educators, we have satisfied ourselves to be strictly reasonable – mere descriptions

---

*For this horror see McPhail, 1972, chapter 2ff., and Peters's review in the *Journal of Moral Education,* vol. 3, no. 1, 1973. Innumerable other examples could be given from what are called 'development' or 'research' projects. There is a widespread belief (fantasy) that the right way to establish 'aims' or 'objectives' is simply to ask the consumers (pupils, teachers, parents, etc.), and the right way to 'evaluate' success is to determine whether the consumers are satisfied, whether what is done is 'popular', cf. Wilson, 1975, pp. 98ff.

of what in fact goes on are, *per se*, of no use. (Not, of course, the *only* reason why psychology and the social sciences are in a mess, but an important one. For other problems see Wilson, 1972a and Harré and Secord, 1972.) 'The task of showing at least some such standards to be reasonable is not, in fact, at all difficult. We *know*, for instance, that children should be taught to read and write 'properly: that they should not get away with playing truant, bullying, vandalism and gross laziness; that they need a reasonably firm disciplinary structure; that they need to be understood and helped as people ('loved' is a fair word for this). Yet even these simple and agreed aims obviously require a school structure which is a good deal more 'potent' than is common, which is much more under the control of those who know the children (the teachers), and which is nothing like so subject to regulations and pressures from bureaucrats, certain types of 'home background', educational fashion, or other social forces.

This perhaps goes a little way to justify a strong suspicion that either we do not entertain any serious educational ideals or we make no serious attempt to realize them in practice. The kind of weight we can give to the term 'serious' I have briefly touched on earlier (see p. 3ff.); but the present impotence of schools does suggest that most of what is said and done here has the quality of fantasy, rather than of any sincere and clear-headed attempt to do the job. Of course the fantasy is assisted and encouraged by difficulties which are, in a broad sense, 'political': how do we get politicians and bureaucrats to relinquish their power, teachers to overcome their deference and take control, parents to insist on potent rather than impotent schools? I do not say that these questions are easily answered. But if all those concerned with education were at least to reach the stage of asking them, something substantial would have been achieved.

Chapter three

Discipline

In the last chapter we spoke of a possible failure of nerve in education, a refusal to face and put into practice certain necessary concepts and principles which are connected with the nature of education itself. Some of these principles are located in an area marked by such terms as 'discipline', 'control', 'keeping order', etc., and it is no accident that this is also an area in which some of the most serious day-to-day worries of practising teachers crop up. In this chapter we shall have a look at one concept, which I take to be normally marked by 'discipline' and which has (so far as I can see) been almost entirely overlooked by contemporary writers, even though a great deal has been said under this title. Entries indexed under the heading (fifteen pages in all) in *Ethics and Education* (Peters, 1966, p. 326), for instance, are in my view not specifically about discipline at all but about other notions, cognate or overlapping, perhaps, but certainly not coextensive.

I can hope to make good this somewhat brusque claim only by implication, during the argument of this chapter; for it is not easy to pin particular authors down. Peters, for instance, says (1966, p. 267):

'Discipline', etymologically speaking, is rooted in a learning situation; it conveys the notion of submission to rules or some kind of order. . . . Whenever we think about rules or a system of order from the point of view of their impression on a mind or minds it is appropriate to talk of 'discipline'. 'Discipline' is thus a very general notion which is connected with conforming to rules.

This is the nearest I can find to a direct statement of what discipline is: but it is not very near, particularly since there is an uncertain interweaving of (a) etymology, (b) contemporary usage amongst English-speakers, and (c) purely conceptual considerations which may or may not co-extend with (a) and (b). Off-hand, one feels inclined to say that we do not speak of 'discipline' in anything like *all* cases of a 'learning situation'

33

or 'conforming to rules', still less of 'a system of order': the notion of discipline is not as 'general' as that. But all this requires much more argument: I do not say the account is wrong, but it is itself too general to be of much use for our purpose.

It is, however, perhaps not entirely unjust to suggest that the tone of such an account (fairly typical of much that is written in contemporary philosophy of education) may lead to a certain kind of mistake, which is clearly apparent in the work of some other writers. Thus P. S. Wilson (1971) says of a certain 'form of order' that 'it is not achieved merely by submission or obedience to orders in the sense of commands, but by trying to see what the *point* of the orders is. It is a matter of discipline, or in other words of trying to learn what is involved in doing what is being ordered' (ibid., p. 78, his italics here and elsewhere). 'Discipline, then, is educative order. The word 'discipline' refers always [*sic*] to the kind of order involved in trying to reach appropriate standards or follow appropriate rules for engaging in a valued activity' (ibid., p. 79). 'Unless the person being disciplined . . . can see at least something of the valuable point of the proposed order, then he will not submit to it for *its* sake (for its *intrinsic* value). . . . In this case, to say that he is being "externally" *disciplined* sounds to me like a contradiction in terms' (ibid.). (It sounds to me at least a bit nearer to what we mean by 'discipline' in ordinary English.) The whole passage (pp. 77–80) and indeed the whole book are methodologically interesting, because the author frequently abandons any serious attempt to investigate normal usage in an effort to sell a particular educational line. This is not *per se* disastrous: but in practice it may be done with more or less wisdom. Of course it is nice if teachers and pupils are banded together in a common enthusiasm for the pursuit of knowledge; and if somebody wants to use the term 'discipline' for the 'form of order' which prevails under such circumstances there is no law to stop him. But in making this move, the author down-grades something which is nearer to what one would normally call 'discipline' and which he calls 'control'; and this leads him to say wild things like (ibid., p. 78):

> If *all* that the teacher is trying to do (at the start of a lesson, for example) is to 'gain control', then he is almost bound to fail to bring the class to order. . . . It is impossible to get thirty or forty children simultaneously quiet for more than a moment or so unless *they* can see some point or value in the constraint.

Of course this might be made (analytically) true if we allow 'point or value' to include things like not getting beaten, dismissed from school, etc. But that is just to say that children are bound to have *some* kind of reason for keeping quiet or enduring the 'constraint', and this is clearly not what the author is trying to say.

Now we all know perfectly well (including the author) that — given the requisite amount of power, sanctions, charisma, or whatever may be contingently required — 'control' is quite enough to keep lots of children quiet both at the start of the lesson and at other times. The point is, he doesn't *like* this sort of thing, and hence wants it to be impossible; hence also wants to make 'discipline' stand for a 'form of order' which he does like. This is a perennial temptation in philosophy, and the author is in excellent company (arguably Plato did something like this with *dikaiosune* in the *Republic*, 433ff.). One's suspicion here is that many 'liberal' or 'progressive-minded' philosophers want to stress, not just any 'learning situation', but the particular (perhaps rather rare) 'learning situation' in which the learners see what is to be learned as in some sense 'intrinsically' valuable: and that they are prepared to monopolize words like 'discipline' in order to advance their cause. But this is cheating.

What has gone wrong here, I think, derives from trying too hard to make a conceptual unity out of an etymological one. We start with 'a learning situation' and end with 'conforming to rules', somehow hoping for a tie-up somewhere in the middle. But clearly a large number of rules that operate where 'discipline', 'well-disciplined' etc., are most at home — in an army, for instance — have no very direct connection with *learning* at all: and conversely, there is an artificiality in the attempt to connect all instances of learning with 'submission to rules' in any way tight enough to give 'discipline' a natural home. But be all this as it may: there is a limit on what may be gained by these linguistic methods, particularly when applied negatively. I am concerned primarily with (if you like) *one* notion that may be — I think, normally is — marked by 'discipline', as the word is commonly used by English speakers in general and by teachers in particular. I shall argue not (or not only) that this notion has the best linguistic or philosophical right, so to speak, to be attached to 'discipline' but also that there are very important substantive and practical reasons why it should be hived off from other notions connected with rule-following, clarified in its own right, and properly understood — particularly by teachers.

In empirical studies by psychologists, sociologists and others the concept seems (so far as I can see) to have vanished completely, at least in the work of contemporary authors. This seems to have infected philosophers; and I shall leave aside some excellent remarks in Kant's writings on education, and begin with the least indirect attempt to deal with *this* notion of discipline that I can find in any serious contemporary philosophical writing. The authors have been dealing with 'discipline' along Peters's lines, 'considered as intimately connected with specific things that have to be learnt', and immediately continue (Hirst and Peters, 1970, p. 127)

More usually, perhaps, in a school context it is used to refer to the maintenance of general conditions of order without which nothing can be effectively learnt. It is connected with children being brought, by various forms of persuasion and coercion, to accept rules forbidding them to make too much noise, to fight in class, to be rude to the teacher, and so on. Without such general conditions of order teaching cannot go on.

Now there are a number of different distinctions we shall want to make in this area; but one broad or overall distinction at least must be enforced, between whatever may be meant by pupils being well-*disciplined* on the one hand, and various notions of the pupils being well-*controlled*, well-ordered, organized, or trouble-free on the other. The first sentence in the quotation above blurs this difference altogether; in the second sentence the phrase 'accept rules' looks more hopeful (surely being well-disciplined is something specifically to do with accepting rules): but then the rules appear to be only 'forbidding them' to do various things, and at the end we are back to 'general conditions of order'. We have also the mistake already noted, that discipline must be about learning and teaching: but this is plainly false even for schools (consider the discipline required for fire-drills, or to maintain good relationships with the local community). One feels here, as so often in educational writing, that the authors are more concerned with what they think the point or purpose of discipline ought to be than with what discipline *is*.

Consider first the notion of a group of people or an institution being well-*organized* for a particular purpose. One can have a well-organized classroom, or army, or operating theatre, or youth camp: this has to do with the *arrangements*, perhaps even more specifically with what one might call the *administrative* arrangements, which facilitate the purpose. A youth camp is badly-organized if the latrines are too far away (or too near): an operating theatre, if it is not arranged that the assistant with the scalpel stands near enough to the surgeon: a classroom, if the desks do not give the children a clear view of the blackboard. To describe all this under the heading 'discipline' is palpably absurd. Now consider the notion of being trouble-free, or in a broad sense 'controlled'. We get trouble-free prisoners by putting them in chains; trouble-free children by slipping them tranquillizers; trouble-free surgical assistants, perhaps, by paying them enough for them not to worry about their mortgages during the operation. Again, this has nothing specifically to do with discipline. And we could run similar arguments with other notions applicable to groups of people: 'having high morale', 'enthusiastic', 'interested', and so on.

'Accepting rules' is much nearer the target, because it brings in the notion of *obedience*. When we talk about the discipline of (say) an army being good, we are not talking about whether its administrative arrangements are good, or whether the soldiers are trouble-free and quiescent, or whether their morale and enthusiasm are high — though all these may, contingently, affect discipline or reflect it. We are talking about whether they obey the rules. Perhaps something more than that, however: whether they can be *relied on* to obey the rules. Suppose we have soldiers who do obey the rules, only they do so rather slothfully and mutter curses under their breath and so on. Well, that is better than not obeying them, and certainly they are more well-*disciplined* than soldiers who conduct wildly enthusiastic charges against the enemy on their own initiative. But we might think that their discipline was a bit suspect, or 'about to crack', or 'slack', or something like that. We are not just concerned with their overt obedience, but with some kind of disposition to obey.

We are already far away from the idea of 'maintenance of general conditions of order' without which some activity (teaching, fighting) 'cannot go on', and far away also from any idea that all the rules we want them to obey are of the general form 'don't cause trouble'. A soldier *qua* soldier has of course to obey some rules which have this sort of point (not getting drunk, malingering, etc.); but he also has duties of a different kind — to make himself a good marksman, be able to read a map, etc. Fighting can go on all right without these; but he would not be a well-disciplined soldier if he did not obey whatever rules enjoined these duties on him: just as a pupil would not be a well-disciplined pupil if he did not make a sufficient effort, at least, to do the work he had been ordered to do. It is perhaps worth noting that we should describe some armies as 'well-disciplined' in virtue of their obedience even to rules which in fact made them *less* efficient fighters: for example, keeping uniforms bright and conspicuous when they would be better off dirty or in camouflage or marching in column when they would suffer less casualties if they spread out. Of course those who made the rules, being in the fighting business, presumably *thought* that obedience to them would make better soldiers —though even this is doubtful: but that is strictly irrelevant — being well-disciplined means obeying the rules *whatever* their relation to fighting.

Can we sharpen up the vagueness of 'some kind of disposition to obey'? First, of course, the well-disciplined soldier will not obey just anyone — he will obey the established authority (his commanders or military regulations); and naturally there can sometimes be a question about what or who *is* the established authority. More difficult, but crucial, is whether he must have certain *reasons* for his obedience. Granted that he obeys consistently, and obeys the established authorities, does it matter why he obeys? He must, of course, obey for *some* kind of reason and in some degree of consciousness; if, for instance, he was just reacting to a set of post-hypnotic commands, that would not suffice to call him 'well-disciplined'; and indeed we might wonder whether to allow this as a fully-fledged case of obeying — it is rather more like animals obeying. But what kind of reasons must he use?

Suppose a Roman legion obeys Caesar consistently, but when Pompey takes it over the troops immediately grow slack and perhaps mutinous. We investigate and find that they obeyed Caesar because of his personal charm, not because he was the legitimate general: Pompey is also legitimate, but charmless. Were they well-disciplined under Caesar? A science class is well-disciplined when in the hands of Mr X because they admire him and of Miss Y because they are in love with her, but disobedient with Mr Z because they hate him. Is the science class a well-disciplined class? Are they well-disciplined even with Mr X and Miss Y? It seems possible that we can say 'yes' or 'no' to these questions, as we wish: which is a bit alarming.

One is tempted here to make Aristotle's move (*Nicomachean Ethics*, Book 2, Thomson, 1955, p. 62) to say that: in a loose sort of way we *call* people 'well-disciplined' (or 'just', or 'kind', or all sorts of things) when their overt behaviour — so long as it has *some* sort of reason — is of a certain kind; but 'really' the well-disciplined (just, kind, etc.) person has to have a particular type of reason. If we make this move, we then go on to specify the type of reason in each case. In the case of discipline, the point would be that the person must obey the rules *because they are authoritative.* This is importantly different from obeying them because they happen to issue from an admired source; but it is also importantly different from obeying them because they are good rules, or sensible rules, or rules required for the purposes of the institution — a feature of rules constantly stressed in the literature but irrelevant to the particular notion of discipline.

It is essential to get this straight, whether we make the move or not. One reason is that we may otherwise be tempted to a kind of behaviourist fantasy into which some psychologists seem actually to have fallen. Observing that the overt behaviour of people, behaviour that might loosely be labelled 'kind' or 'altruistic' or whatever, varies enormously according to the particular context, some researchers seem to deny that there is any such thing as 'altruism'; altruism is said not to be 'a unitary trait' (Wilson, 1973, p. 79). This conclusion derives from the idea that all we can do is to observe external behaviour (never mind the antecedent reasons for it). But of course there is such a thing as following a particular rule or syllogism such as 'be kind to other people because they are human beings, whatever the context'; and it would be very odd indeed if some men did not follow such a rule better than others. If in fact they do not — and to determine this we should have to determine their reasons for action in each context — then this is certainly interesting and shows that they do not perhaps, have a clear concept of kindness or altruism at all. In the same way, if pupils' overt obedience-behaviour varied entirely according to the teacher and other contextual features, one might want to say that they had not really got hold of the notion of discipline *at all*.

And this would be a very important conclusion, whether or not one chose to make Aristotle's move. For (whatever we may want to do about the *words*) there is clearly a particular concept at stake here: roughly, the notion of *obedience to established and legitimate authorities as such*. One could say a very great deal about the practical importance of grasping this notion and making it part of one's life and behaviour; indeed, it is difficult to see how, without this, any institution or society can do more than rely upon the *ad hoc* variety of bribes or threats that might get things done — Mr X's charm, Miss Y's beautiful appearance, payment for doing good homework, electric shocks, or whatever else we may wish to deploy. But quite apart from any question of the inefficiency or fragility of such pressures, to omit the notion of discipline in this sense is to omit a whole swathe of concepts (authority, punishment, contract, law and so on) which are logically inevitable for rational creatures (see chapter 3).

What is it, though, to accept rules as 'authoritative'? What is it to obey something or somebody as a source of authority rather than just a source of power? I do not want to retrace ground already covered tolerably well by other writers (Peters, 1966, p. 246, with reference to Winch, 1959—60); but there are some particular points to be made in relation to the notion of being well-disciplined. We have somehow to tread a middle way between two ideas, neither of which coextend with the idea of discipline, which I shall call 'total consent' and 'submission to power'. Some examples:

1   Roman soldiers were (sometimes) well-disciplined if anyone ever was. But it would be grotesque to say that they had always given anything like free or total consent to their authorities, or had in some way freely contracted to abide by the rules. Many of them had been economically forced, conned, lured or press-ganged into service. Their good discipline plainly did not depend on a totally *free* acceptance, nor on their acceptance of the rules, commanders, campaigns, or anything else as necessarily *good* or desirable.

2   On the other hand, we cannot regard their behaviour — at those times when, and to the extent that, such behaviour was well-disciplined — as in any simple or direct way *forced*. They were not well-disciplined when their centurions had to cudgel them in order to get them to perform various tasks: my behaviour is not well-disciplined if I advance only because there is a sword in my back. Such behaviour may be in accordance with the rules in

force, but my reason for so behaving is not to obey the rules. My thought is not 'I will advance, or else I shall have failed in my duty', but 'I will advance, or else I shall get stabbed'.

To accept rules as authoritative, in the sense required for discipline, consists partly in accepting them as *reasons for action*; and this is verified by whether, in the practical situations involved, the motivating thought is something like 'it's a rule' rather than anything else — for example 'it's a good idea', 'I shall suffer if I don't obey', 'I like doing this sort of thing', etc. Whether this is in fact what I have called the 'motivating thought' can, at least in principle, be established by setting up enough controlled situations in which the irrelevant variables do not apply: we see how the subject thinks and acts when it is a bad rule, when he will not suffer for disobedience, and so on.

Discipline is concerned with the consistency and strength of these on-the-spot acceptances or cases of obedience to authority. This of course involves or presumes his overall acceptance of the authority as such: but it does not involve any question about *why* he accepts it. There may be all kinds of reasons why a person accepts or submits to a source of power. I may do this in something like total freedom, as perhaps when I decide to learn French and put myself in the hands of a French teacher. Or, more commonly, I may think that the existing political authorities, rotten though they are, represent the only practically desirable alternative at the present time, and so consent to their rules. Or I may simply find myself (perhaps more commonly still) in a situation where I have no immediate means of escape from the authorities or powers-that-be, and opt to 'play their game' either because it is the best I can do for myself or because of mere inertia. Many other possibilities exist. The analogy with games, weak at some points, is here strong; why a person plays in the first place (and his general outlook on the game as a whole) is one thing; his detailed obedience to the rules as such, another.

Of course not all these rules are of the same kind, or stem from the same authority. A lot here turns on the subject of which 'well-disciplined' is predicated. Thus we conceive of a soldier, for the most part, as one who obeys the orders of others, these orders being represented in a fairly concrete form; so long as he does what his superiors tell him, and obeys regulations laid down in some manual or rule-book, he is well-disciplined. It is not required that he should, on his *own* initiative, improve his marksmanship or map-reading — that (for a soldier) shows him to be keener or more dedicated, but not better-disciplined. A soldier's *duty* begins and ends with obedience to others. A well-disciplined chess-player, or athlete, or swordsman, on the other hand, obeys rules inherent in his *techne*: such people are not just occupiers of roles, but also craftsmen. The chess-player restrains his eagerness in deference to principles concerned with building up an adequate defence before attacking, the athlete paces himself rather than just running flat out, and so on.

Pace the Latin derivation, it is today a little odd to use 'well-disciplined' even in such cases, just as it is odd to talk of someone as 'well-disciplined' in his moral relationships with other people. Perhaps this is because 'discipline' is most at home when closely connected with fairly clear-cut *social roles* and situations — in an army, in an operating theatre, in a class-room, on a ship. The demands we make under 'discipline' seem pretty down-to-earth; thus we may say of a citizen who pays his taxes, keeps the peace, etc., that he is law-abiding, but not that he is well-disciplined. Now put him in ancient Sparta, where his life is much more a matter of quasi-military obligation, and the word becomes more natural. Most natural of all is its use not of an individual, but of a group: it is not, or certainly not primarily, Smith minor or Private Jones or Amompharetus who are well-disciplined, but the Lower Fifth, the Second Battalion, and the Spartan army. Individuals are more likely to be described as simply 'disobedient'.

This does not imply, of course, anything about the *constitutional* basis (as one might call it) of the group. Roles, tasks and duties may be allotted democratically — I mean, as a result of discussion and majority vote — or by a dictator. Discipline prevails when these duties are carried out in obedience to the rules: constitutional questions about who makes the rules, what methods there are of changing them, etc., are here irrelevant. It is perhaps a contingent fact that social groups who operate democratically *create* fewer contexts in which it is appropriate to speak of 'discipline' than do less democratic groups: that is, fewer contexts in which there are those quasi-military obligations that make the word natural. For example, a ship's company which had a democratic constitution, on which everyone participated in decision-making, would in practice be more suited to a pleasure-cruise than a battle; and we should not speak so easily of 'discipline' on a pleasure-cruise. But it would be possible (as in some instances during the later Peloponnesian War, in the Athenian navy) for a ship or a fleet to change its constitution in the direction of democracy, at least to some degree, and still to operate in contexts where 'discipline' is relevant — that is, of course, by continuing to allot roles and tasks in a military style.

We can go further on these lines with the notions of 'task' and 'authority'. For 'discipline', 'well-disciplined', etc., to be in place, the task has to be a fairly specific or practical one. It is not a matter of *discipline* whether I, as a Christian, obey the authority of priest or scriptures in such matters as forgiving my enemies, loving my neighbour, and so on; on the other hand, it would be so if as a monk I obey or disobey more specific instructions, emanating from the abbot or the rules of my order. Similarly revolutionaries may be praised for ordering their lives according to the precepts of say, Marx; but they are only praised for being well-disciplined in so far as they obey the orders of the revolutionary leader or committee. Being, in general, a good Christian or a good Marxist is not a task in the required sense.

But equally the task must be specific *to* the authority and the group: not just any obedience to accepted authority will do. A local policeman may often issue commands to the citizens in his neighbourhood; but the citizens' obedience is not a case of good discipline in the way that the obedience of the policeman's subordinates in the police force would be. The citizens are under the policeman's authority but not, one might say, under his discipline. So too a teacher *qua* adult may give orders to children; but whether or not such orders can be regarded as authoritative, obedience to them is only a matter of discipline if the children are a working group under his particular authority for a particular purpose — if, that is, he gives his orders *qua* the teacher of a particular class of pupils or at least *qua* a teacher in the school of which they are members.

Obviously a group can be well-disciplined in respect of one authority and badly-disciplined in respect of another; for instance, the members of a revolutionary organization. Similarly, pupils' behaviour may be guided by the authority of their peer-group or gang, or even perhaps of the school bully, rather than that of the teacher. We should often have difficulty in deciding whether we could sensibly talk of 'authority' here, rather than just 'power' or 'influence': clearly authority requires something in the way of formal recognition or acceptance ('legitimization'), and has to be to some degree institutionalized. But it is plain that two or more potential authorities might compete for obedience, even within the fairly narrow sphere demarcated by 'discipline'.

Finally, there will be some occasions on which we should hesitate to use 'well-disciplined' or 'badly-disciplined' at all; not now because the kind of task or authority is logically inappropriate, but more simply because obedience is either non-existent or so negligible that the terms are out of place. The notion of discipline involves some presumption that the group is meant to be, and is minimally trying to be, obedient; some *expectation* of obedience. A continuing total lack of such obedience would extinguish such expectation; if pupils constantly paid no serious attention to the teacher at all, we should not say that they were badly-disciplined or even that the discipline was appalling, we should say rather that there was no discipline at all.

It would be possible, and no doubt desirable, to map out the scope of discipline in still more detail; but perhaps it is already clear enough, for our purposes, to make it worth while linking it with the assessment of pupils as more or less well-disciplined. We saw earlier the plausibility of bringing under this heading the notion of *reasons* for obedience as well as the more obvious notion of overt obedience (for any reason). It is important to see that these reasons may not only be more or less operative in behaviour, but also more or less *fragile* in themselves. One might object to speaking of 'fragility', on the grounds that a man's reason for obeying must be either of one kind or of another, that is, either the thought 'it's a rule' is what motivates him, or some other (irrelevant) thought. This (as we suggested earlier) could in principle be settled by a sufficient number of test cases. 'So it is not a matter of such a thought or principle being "fragile": either it is operative or it is not. We can score the man for consistency (how *often* it operates) but not for "fragility".' I think this is over-simple, because it seems clear that human beings have competing thoughts or motives: 'it's a rule' can coexist in a man's mind with 'I don't want to obey, it's unpleasant', 'it doesn't stem from a nice person', or whatever. Whether or not a particular motivating thought issues in behaviour, it can be of greater or lesser strength, more or less fragile, that is, more or less liable to be upset by other countervailing thoughts. Its strength could, in principle, be verified (the man's degree of remorse or regret, and other symptoms, would be relevant here) other than by external behaviour.

In fact, there may be very little correlation with behaviour. Some pupils, for instance, may have a very strong motivating thought 'it's a rule', and yet fail to translate this into behaviour because, perhaps, they are frightened of their peer-group: other pupils, less frightened, may have the same thought in a much weaker form and behave in accordance with it. We would not, of course, describe the former as 'well-disciplined', because the behaviour is lacking; but the latter lack *one* element of being well-disciplined to a degree that the former do not lack it – that is, a strong adherence to the idea 'it's a rule'. That there is *some* conceptual connection between principles and behaviour does not imply that we cannot assess the various aspects of discipline independently (cf. Wilson, 1973, part 2 and 1971, pp. 135ff.).

Add the importance of reasons to what we saw earlier about the scope of discipline, and we gain something which is of particular relevance to practical teaching: that is, an idea of discipline as an educational objective in its own right – not just as a facilitator for education. One might perhaps categorize it under moral or political education. It involves the understanding and practice of a particular virtue, confined to particular types of situation which are nevertheless of great practical importance: roughly, situations which are 'tight' enough (I have used the word 'quasi-military') for us to want to speak of 'discipline' as against more general terms such as 'law-abiding'. This has very little to do with notions vaguely canvassed under such headings as 'autonomy', 'self-discipline', and others, and has to be sharply separated from them.

There are reasons why this particular educational objective is important, and why it is currently in dispute. Briefly, it will appear, to liberally-minded adults in a civilized, peaceful and pluralistic society, as if the number of tightly-structured, quasi-military situations in which our pupils are likely to find themselves is small, and as if such situations were either not very important or positively objectionable (perhaps as leading to 'conformism' or 'authoritarianism', or whatever). Conversely, there are those who are naturally predisposed to such situations, and who will instinctively favour increasing them (one thinks here of demands to reintroduce military service, perhaps of sail training, Outward Bound courses, and so on). Leaving prejudice aside, however, we need to note:

1 It is inevitable that children are born and will spend some years in a situation which is tightly-structured in the way described. The family is a group of this kind: so is the classroom and the school as a whole. Notions like obedience, duties, allotted tasks, and so on, are here inexpellable notions. If a child did not grasp and act upon the principle of discipline, of obedience to established authority, he could hardly survive at all: and a proper grasp of it is an essential enablement for the child to learn other things.

2 Because of this, 'discipline' — although *per se* only one subheading of the general area of contractual obligation, acting out of principle, rule-following and so forth — is inevitably a crucially important area. The family and the school necessarily form the arena of the child's first encounter with the whole business of rules and authority; if he does not grasp the relevant points in this arena, it is unlikely (certain developmentalists might say, impossible) that he will do so later when he comes to wider and less structured contexts in which the word 'discipline' is less applicable.

3 Although not many social groups are 'military', a great many are more like a peace-time army than they are like (say) a university or a collection of bohemian artists. We may legitimately speak of 'discipline' in groups of people building bridges, making cars, digging coal, trawling for fish, and a large number of other cases. It is clear enough that — be our or any other society as 'liberal' as it may — we should not survive very long without adequate discipline in such contexts. And these are the contexts in which most of our pupils will in fact operate.

The contrast between discipline, in the sense outlined, and the quite different notion of being 'controlled' or 'trouble-free', is one which teachers (whether they know it or not) face every day. Not infrequently it produces a conflict of aims. Given sufficient charm, bribes, rewards, etc. — or just the willingness to overlook offences — it may be possible to keep a class of pupils trouble-free; if we insist on discipline, we may create more trouble rather than less. (Just as, in some industrial situations, it pays the management to 'square' their workers by any means possible, without worrying about contractual obligations or fair play or anything of that kind: or just as, if you wished to survive as a Roman emperor, you gave donatives to the troops, regardless of whether they *deserved* it.) Many teachers are in a position where they are doing well if they can survive; it seems a bit much to ask them to take on discipline as well. If they let offenders get away with it, who shall blame them? Bribe the bully, let the tiresome child play truant, put the badly-behaved out of the room if absolutely necessary, overlook the rule-breaker, turn a blind eye to the lazy and thank God for the end of term.

Together with the absence of conceptual clarity about discipline, unsurprisingly, goes the absence of any serious support for teachers in the task of enforcing and teaching discipline. Here we go back to the notion of *control*, perhaps the best word to use for the most fundamental requirements of any social group. If anything is to *be done* or not be done — with no worries, for the moment, about reasons which people use for doing or not doing it — then there must be ways of ensuring that it is done: 'control' may stand for these ways. 'Control' may, as we have seen, operate by all sorts of methods: hypnosis, electric shocks, terror, bribery, drugs, conditioning, appeals to reason, and so on — including, of course, the straightforward use of force (as when we pick a child up and simply carry him to bed). The teacher must have enough methods of control at his disposal to get done what he wants done or, more simply, he must have enough *power*. Without this he cannot be sure of achieving any of his objectives: and this includes the sophisticated objectives of turning out pupils who may be described (vaguely) as 'autonomous', 'rational', 'independent', 'free-thinking', 'critical' and so on. Indeed, the more sophisticated the objective, the more power and methods of control he is likely to need. It is an obvious fallacy to suppose that 'liberal' aims entail 'liberal' ('democratic', etc.) methods alone (see chapter 4, pp. 56ff.).

Important questions may be raised about the conceptual and empirical connection between methods of control and the learning of discipline: an area largely unexplored because of the naive assumptions (if we may dignify them by that word) that they are the same thing anyway, and even if they are not, our aims and methods in both areas ought to have the same flavour (so to speak) — 'free', 'liberal', 'strict', or whatever the prevailing taste may be. Some of these questions I have tried to clarify in another place (Wilson, 1972b). What I want to stress here is that serious *educational* objectives, and in particular the teaching of discipline, necessarily require a great deal more control (power) than the teacher usually has available. For clearly the teacher will want to try out such things as: getting pupils to make up and obey their own rules, putting them in contexts of obedience which vary in different dimensions (different types of authority, different specific rules, different types of enforcement, different styles of obedience, etc.), clarifying and 'making real' the concepts involved not only by direct instruction but also by role-play, impromptu drama, simulated situations and so on — and no doubt the imaginative teacher will be able to think of many more practical methods.

Now this requires much more than might be meant by 'control' in some such phrase as 'keeping control' ('maintaining order', etc.). It is not only a question of 'general conditions of order' without which 'teaching cannot go on' (Hirst and Peters, 1970, p. 127). Rather, the teacher needs to be able, at the drop of a hat, to get his orders carried out, to switch pupils rapidly and smoothly from one context to another, and to obtain instant participation in whatever system or rule-structure he thinks desirable. Much of this will be a matter of 'bouncing' pupils into various structures and activities (I use this odd word because I can think of no other which gets the right flavour: 'drill', 'train', 'order', 'initiate', etc. are nowhere near) in something like the way in which a PT instructor or a teacher of impromptu dramatics often does — 'Right, now it's a dictatorship, X is dictator'; 'Now you're teaching a class of five-year-olds: what rules do you make?' 'OK, I'm one of the class, I break this rule — what do you do?', and so on.

I spell this out in a naive and long-winded way because it is essential to see that the teacher needs to have the pupils 'in the hollow of his hand' rather than just 'in hand'. For many this is an alarming picture, generating words like 'totalitarian', 'tyranny', and so on. But it is a necessary one, and contrasts strongly with a picture of the teacher as not much more than a one-man Noise Abatement Society. This applies, of course, to other forms of learning than learning discipline — much of moral education in general, as well as other things, will need this kind of treatment. There is a sort of vicious circle here: unless and until the teacher can exercise this sort of 'control' (if we must call it that), one is tempted to say, he cannot teach them discipline: and he cannot exercise such control fully, at least, unless and until they are tolerably well-disciplined.

This makes it all the more important to place as much stress as possible, or at least as necessary, upon direct *obedience* to the teacher, his *authority*, and the efficiency of the sanctions required to back it up. It seems that such obedience must first be established, whatever reasons the pupil may have for obeying: on that the teacher can then build, improving the pupil's reasons and conceptual grasp. For reasons into which we need not enquire, obedience is still extremely unfashionable: the term is not often used, perhaps partly because it represents a concept less easy to avoid than what I have taken to be the central concept marked by 'discipline'. It is no part of philosophy to suggest what individual or political action should be taken, or by whom, in order to recover these concepts and put them back to work in educational practice; but it is, I think, tolerably clear that some such action is urgently required.

Chapter four

Authority

The general questions raised at the end of the last chapter about 'authority' and concepts connected with it are, I think, of great practical importance for teachers. For though the individual teacher may not by himself be able to change the various laws and regulations which affect his job (the truancy laws, for instance, or his legal rights in the area of discipline and punishment), yet in practice he has a good deal of latitude. He can try to enforce, or turn a blind eye, and more generally, his acceptance or rejection of particular views of 'authority' will often determine what actually goes on in schools — particularly what goes on by way of educating pupils in relation to these concepts, as we saw in the case of 'discipline'.

It needs first to be shown that we are dealing here with a set of inter-connected concepts — 'authority', 'rules', 'punishment', 'institutions', and others — which mark, as I see it, logically inevitable or inexpellable features of human social life or interaction: concepts which are bound to have *some* application or instantiation, and which it will be both senseless and unnecessary to 'challenge', 'question', or 'justify' *in general.* This view stands in fairly sharp contrast to a good deal of philosophical literature; and the contrast is particularly evident in relation to one of these notions, the notion of *punishment.* For fairly obvious reasons, this notion has caused a good deal of soul-searching among the tender-minded, and forms a good point of entry. Thus Peters, in a section entitled 'The justification of punishment' (1966, p. 169):

> Punishment, then is retributive by definition. It is part of the meaning of the term that it must involve pain or unpleasantness and that it must be as a consequence of an offence. . . . It is not a law of nature that if people commit offences pain is inflicted on them. This happens regularly only because men have instituted legal systems which ordain that offenders will have pain inflicted on them. People brought up under such systems therefore tend to make this retributive

relationship hold. But the question has to be faced by rational men whether it is appropriate both that pain should be inflicted when a rule is broken and that it should necessarily be inflicted on and only on the person who has broken the rule. How can these normative demands built into the concept of 'punishment' be justified? . . . The answer given to this question will depend, of course, on the general ethical theory which a man adopts.

Similarly Hirst and Peters (1970, p. 128):

'Punishment', in its central cases, has at least three logically necessary conditions. . . .
  i. It must involve the intentional infliction of pain or of some kind
     of unpleasantness.
 ii. This must be inflicted on an offender as a consequence of a
     breach of rules.
iii. It must be inflicted by someone in authority. . . . This introduces
     the question of the justification of punishment.

In general, a utilitarian line is taken, according to which 'Punishment is a necessary mischief, the lesser of two evils' (ibid., p. 129).

This picture has certain internal oddities and obscurities. Thus it is odd to make pain a central notion here: comparatively few punishments involve pain. Even 'unpleasantness' seems not strictly necessary: how far convicted people find (say) prison pleasant or unpleasant — how far they *enjoy* it or *like* it — does not seem to be central: the point is rather that this is something enforced on them whether they like it or not. Again, 'as a consequence of' hardly makes us clearer: if I beat a boy who has broken a rule, and we want to know whether this is meant (or taken) as punishment or shock treatment, nothing is gained by saying that it is done 'as a consequence of', 'because of', or 'for' the breach of rule. The sense of 'for' which we need is actually very hard to elucidate: it is certainly nearer to 'in return for' than 'as a consequence of'. (Try paraphrasing 'for' in 'three for a shilling', 'I'll get you for this', 'he paid for it', 'the French for "dog" ', 'a medal for bravery', etc. 'Retribution' does not make anything much clearer.) These oddities are, I think, symptomatic of a picture of punishment as a contingent and prima facie highly objectionable phenomenon. Now contrast the following argument:

1 Anything that could seriously be called a 'society' or 'social group', as against a collection of hermits who happen to be living in the same area, involves some kind of interaction between its mem-bers; and 'interaction' here will not mean just that they bump up against each other like physical objects, but that they engage in some

rule-following activity — even if, as perhaps in the case of a seminar or a tea-party, the activity consists only or chiefly of linguistic communication. There will therefore be rules or norms which are commonly subscribed to, whether or not they are codified, overtly agreed and stated beforehand, or contracted for.

2 A breach of these rules must, at least characteristically if not in every case, be taken to entail the enforcement of some disadvantage on the breaker. If this were not so, we should not be able to identify them as rules prohibiting X and enjoining Y, rather than enjoining X and prohibiting Y: or else we should not be able to identify them as rules at all, as against wishes, pious hopes, generalizations about human behaviour, or descriptions of some other-worldly ideal. A social rule enjoining X exists only if, when people fail to perform X, something which is characteristically a disadvantage is normally enforced on them.

3 Various words may be in place for the *type* of 'disadvantage' — 'punishment', 'penalty', 'sanctions', etc., as well as for the *form* of 'disadvantage' — 'ostracism', 'imprisonment', 'exile'. Not all these disadvantages will be *painful* (going to prison does not involve pain), but they will all be characteristically 'bad things', otherwise they would not be disadvantages but rewards. Thus loss of liberty is, characteristically, a 'bad thing'; though a man may sometimes, even often, find a situation where he is told what to do is more pleasant than a situation where he can do what he wants he must in general wish to retain the option of liberty so long as he continues to see himself as a human agent. (This is why 'unpleasant' is not quite right.) Further, whether or not the group gives some of its members particular authority to interpret and enforce the rules and disadvantages, the disadvantages will in every case occur by reason or in virtue of the rules that constitute and govern the group's interaction. That the group subscribes to these rules, or that the rules are in force, logically entails disadvantages to rule-breakers, whether or not these disadvantages are properly called 'punishments' inflicted by special authorities.

4 In English we speak of 'punishment' in reference to the common and criminal law, and in reference to some institutions with limited sovereignty (for example, schools). With games, and (perhaps) generally in cases where we wish to avoid the implication of moral blame, we prefer to speak of 'penalties': elsewhere we may talk of 'sanctions' or more vaguely of 'being made to suffer for' a breach of rules (for example, of social etiquette). Other languages may not make these distinctions, which may indeed sometimes seem arbitrary: *poena* in Latin, for instance, covers a wider range than our 'punishment'. The question thus arises of whether we are trying to 'justify punishment' in reference

to the particular (and, it may be thought, in some degree arbitrary) range of instances for which we use the word 'punishment' (and not 'penalty', 'sanctions' etc.), or whether we are to 'justify' some more general concept.

5 If some more general concept is at stake, it is presumably the concept of being (as I have called it) 'disadvantaged' in virtue of rules governing social interaction. But we have seen that such disadvantaging is logically entailed by the notion of social interaction. What could it mean to 'justify punishment (disadvantaging)'? I suppose some such question as 'Why should we have any form of social interaction and rules at all?' might be coherently raised (though I doubt this), but it would be necessary to raise such a question in order to make any sense of 'justifying punishment' *as a whole*. More probably a person who, in real life, protests against or demands justification for punishment objects to one or other of the *kinds* of punishments, or rules, or authorities, or systems in force: but this is a different story. He may also be led to raise questions about the whole conceptual apparatus of which punishment is a part – the whole 'basis of authority', as it might be called: and *some* of these questions, as we shall see below, are both intelligible and important. But that too is a different story.

6 If, on the other hand, we are interested solely in the specific concept of punishment as the word is used by English-speakers, it will be difficult to know how to proceed. For suppose that we dismantled the legal system of judges, codified laws, specified penalties and so on, then plainly there would still remain most or at least some of the forms of social interaction, with rules and ensuing disadvantages, even if these disadvantages were not formally administered in courts of law. The same criteria as those commonly listed by philosophers for 'punishment' would pertain: disadvantages would still be given by the social group for breaches of the rules. Whether or not we would continue to *call* these 'punishments' rather than 'penalties', 'sanctions', etc., seems to me an open question, and not a very interesting one. Certainly they might be just as harsh, or perhaps harsher: laws and school rules may be severe, but the sanctions or penalties imposed by mobs, bullies and even the peer group may well be more so. Arguments for or against the specific form of sanctions which seems to be implied by 'punishment' – perhaps a comparatively high degree of formalization, or codification – would be heavily dependent on empirical facts: off-hand one might be inclined to suppose that the degree of institutionalization implied would improve clarity at least, and hence (other things being equal) be a more desirable form than the more unpredictable forces of codified law in general. But however that may be, we are now clearly involved in a discussion of the best *kinds* of sanctions or disadvantages:

not what is commonly taken as 'the justification of punishment'.

What seems to have gone wrong is this. Philosophers of a utilitarian turn of mind have seized on 'the infliction of pain' as something prima facie morally objectionable. Forgetting the conceptual connections we have outlined above, they have then asked 'whether it is appropriate . . . that pain should be inflicted', suggested that 'the answer given to this question will depend on the general ethical theory which a man adopts', and talked about 'the refusal to attach sanctions to socially important rules', as if this were an intelligible empirical possibility. But it is not.*

This perhaps brings a little nearer to the surface a common contemporary attitude which we find in many teachers and educators and social workers already, and which philosophers ought to be curing rather than reinforcing. It is as if Kant's community of angels were regarded as a conceptually coherent ideal. The attitude emerges in such passages as (Peters, 1966, p. 279):

> The truth of the matter is that punishment in a school is at best a necessary nuisance. It is necessary as a deterrent, but its positive educational value is dubious. Education cannot go on unless minimum conditions of order obtain, and punishment may on occasions be necessary in order to ensure such conditions. . . . Under normal conditions [sic] enthusiasm for the enterprise, combined with imaginative techniques of presentation and efficient class management will avert the need for punishment.

In the parallel passage in Hirst and Peters (1970, p. 129), 'under normal conditions' is well replaced by 'ideally'. If one has a concept of punishment which is divorced from the more general idea of sanctions and penalties, and which is tied fairly tight to the notion of pain, then of course this makes a kind of sense. But what we have to remember is that, in so far as there are clear and operative norms or rules, then precisely to that extent failure and breaches will be penalized in *some* way.

Indeed this seems to be more than just a social matter. In so far as I, even alone or on a desert island, seriously propose to myself ends or goals and rules for achieving them, to that extent I shall necessarily blame myself when I fail through my own fault: I shall feel remorse or regret, guilt or shame — we might even talk, more or less metaphorically, of my 'punishing myself'. This goes *together with* 'enthusiasm for the enterprise', not against it or as an alternative strategy to it. Success and

*Cf. Strawson, 1962. Hart (quoted in Peters, 1966, p. 285) says 'This is how human nature in society actually is, and as yet we have no power to alter it.' 'As yet' makes no sense in my view (and, I think in Strawson's).

failure, and hence in a broad sense 'rewards' and 'punishments', are in-expellable from human life. An individual or society may, of course, change the norms (just as, in the way we saw in (6) above, the types of sanctions may be changed); and one way of doing this precisely is to take away their sanctions, which at once *eo ipso* removes their status as norms. For instance, if being a nuisance in school or society character-istically results in a person's receiving more attention and care (support from counsellors and welfare services, and so on) rather than some dis-advantage, then there is no longer an operative norm or rule — though there may be one on paper — against 'being a nuisance'. The norm has in effect become just a pious hope. This sort of situation does, I think, pertain in many schools today: and perhaps also, to no inconsiderable degree, in society at large. It is as if we were no longer sure what ac-tions we wished to bring under the whole mechanism of *justice*; and this may have the effect of making us lose our grip generally on the concept of justice itself and its attendant concepts, of which punish-ment is one.

For much the same reason two other notions (among many), generally marked by the terms 'authority' and 'institution', are also inexpellable. Any society or interacting group of rational creatures must have a common decision-procedure: indeed this can be taken as a defining characteristic of a society (Lucas, 1966, pp. 10ff.). As Peters (1966, p. 238) says, the notion of authority 'presupposes some sort of normative order'. But it is also presupposed by it: and it is not true, as he says in the same context, that 'We can conceive of a society of highly moral beings living together amicably out of respect for a moral law and for each other as rational beings, without anyone being in authority, and without anyone being thought of as an authority.' The reason is not only because men are inherently non-angelic, 'bloody-minded' as Lucas calls it (p. 1), but because in order to *express* their amicable dispositions and 'have respect . . . for each other' such beings would need decision-procedures and authorities to operate them. If you cash out the notion of 'normative order' into actual cases of things that these beings might *do* — exchange goods, play cricket, hold debates, run railways, or whatever — the point becomes clear. Authori-ties (referees, arbitrators, umpires, etc.) are necessary, not just to punish vice, but to provide clarity in those rule-governed activities: 'the editor's decision is final', not or not only because somebody has to mark down incompetent entries, but because it has to be clear what counts as winning the competition. In the same sort of way (the argu-ment need not be put on stage again) the structural contexts which incorporate and clothe these activities — that is, 'institutions' — are also inevitable.

At this point one might stop, and quote 'philosophy leaves every-thing as it is'. Certainly we might say that such considerations as these call certain fantasies (for example, anarchism) into question, or make it more difficult for those who have them to express them as they used to do. Someone who says he wants no rules and punishments *at all*, or the abolition of ('alienating') institutions *in general*, or the complete removal of *any* kind of authority, may now think twice. But to stop here would replace Socratic midwifery by straightforward abortion. People who are morally concerned about punishments, authorities and so on are concerned about *something*, or rather about many things. For there are all sorts of questions we can still raise. I think the most useful thing I can do here is to say something about one or two of the particular questions which are likely to be in the minds of teachers and other educators, in relation to what I have said above.

1 It may still seem as if the conceptual points we have made in this chapter and the previous one convey no more than the bleak message 'you must obey authority'. And does this not have the very unpleasant implications marked by such phrases as 'unquestioning obedience', 'conformism', 'authoritarian regimes', and so on? Does it not lead directly to the horrors perpetrated by those who, like the Nazis, slavishly and uncritically did what they were told? How, then, can we accept these conceptual points (assuming them to be correct) whilst at the same time educating our children to think for themselves and question authority? How can it be possible both to obey and challenge?

It may seem at first sight as if the whole idea of 'questioning authority' is somehow contradictory. If one has authority, the implication is that one is and ought to be, at least characteristically, obeyed *whether or not* one's *particular* commands are thought by the individual to be wise, or pleasant, or on other grounds acceptable. Otherwise there would be no difference between an authority and an adviser. The authority of a ship's captain rests on his being obeyed, at least in regard to the ship's management, irrespective of the views of this or that sailor. There is one sense, therefore, in which 'unquestioning obedience' is required by the very notion of authority: just as such obedience, in certain task-like situations, constitutes part of what it is to be well-disciplined. Certainly if there were too many cases of challenge or disobedience, we should hestitate to say that there was any authority (or any discipline) at all.

But this will only seem alarming and difficult if we persist in regarding 'authority' as equivalent to one particular set of power-holders or 'authorities': rather as a simple-minded person might identify 'morality' with the particular *mores* of his own society, or 'religion' with the particular religious beliefs and institutions with which he happened to be familiar. Of course we can question, challenge, disobey or dispense entirely with these particular manifestations: but we cannot, as I see it, hope to do without some manifestation — not, at least, so long as we remain human beings and interact socially with each other. Just as it is a conceptual truth that human beings must accept some authority and obey it if they are to get anything done, so it is also conceptually true that — if they are indeed human beings, and not robots or zombies — questions will inevitably arise about whether particular authorities are legitimate, whether their scope is properly delimited, whether the form and methods by which they operate is as good as we can make it, and so forth.

This is, or ought to be, entirely familiar ground to us. It is roughly similar to saying that, on the one hand we must abide by whatever the rules of the game are if we are to play games at all: but that, on the other hand, we need sometimes — perhaps often — to think about what sorts of games to play, what rules it would be best to have, whether to have referees or just books of rules, and all the other matters which we need to get straight. Or, again, it is like saying that, on the one hand, there must be some sort of government (sovereign body, set of decision-makers) if we are to act together as a society at all: but that, on the other hand, we need contexts in which we can keep a watching brief on, and often revise, the form or constitution of the government, the delimitation of its sovereignty, or the particular people we want to have as decision-makers.

It is important to note that, even when we engage in this process of reconsideration and revision, we do not thereby step outside of the notion of authority altogether. Suppose that, whilst nominally under the authority of occupying Nazis, we decide to form a resistance movement. Then not only are we proposing to substitute one authority for another (the Free French for the Nazis), rather than to get rid of authority altogether; but also *in the process* of deciding this, of *forming* the movement (with its leaders, rules discipline and so on) we accept some authority. In such a case the authority might be the commands of a particular person (General de Gaulle), or something rather more vague such as 'the will of the French people'. Simply because our activity is collective and purposive, because we are doing things together for a common end, we have to accept some decision-procedure. Again, if pupils in school decided to rebel against the teachers' authority, some other authority would inevitably arise: not only after the success of the rebellion, but in order to carry the rebellion through. Perhaps the pupils would meet and abide by a democratic vote; perhaps they would accept the lead of the strongest and most vociferous. But they would have to accept something.

Of course sensible societies or social groups make proper arrangements for the business of revision. Instead of allowing a free-for-all in which the strongest or most persuasive party is likely to win power, they institutionalize conflicts of opinion and desire: that is, they provide some sort of mechanism or procedure which their members agree to use – for instance, to vote rather than assassinate, or to advance arguments rather than to throw bombs. Agreement about these ultimate decision-procedures is crucial: the alternative to sincere agreement and negotiation within accepted rules being either mindless conformity, or some sort of civil war.

In educating pupils to raise questions and be critical about particular manifestations of authority, the most important thing is to provide proper contexts in which this can be done: or perhaps one should say, to allow and encourage the pupils to create and abide by contexts they themselves opt for – since it is more than half the battle to get them to see that the serious 'questioning of authority' itself involves obedience to rules. The task is to show them, or let them come to grasp, that rules and authority are logically required by human co-operation, and not simply imposed from outside in one particular form by one particular set of people (teachers, or parents, or 'society', or whoever). Success in this task will almost certainly involve giving pupils a good deal of freedom to act out the experiences necessary to grasp the point – though not letting them go so far as the children in Golding's *Lord of the Flies* – rather than just talk about it: serious thinking tends to be promoted by having actual responsibility, and taking the consequences of one's own errors.

2 Are there not, though, some general principles which should guide us (and our pupils) when we are 'questioning authority' in these contexts? What sorts of reasons could we have for setting up one particular manifestation of authority (together with its attendant rules and sanctions) rather than another? Ought our régimes to be more 'democratic' or 'authoritarian', or to involve more 'participation' or 'pupil power'? As these fashionable terms suggest, there are certainly some general pressures – climates of opinion or feeling, as it were – which affect the running of educational institutions in various ways. Can we say anything sensible about all this?

The first and perhaps most important thing to be said is that any overall or *a priori* preference for a particular style or regime – 'authoritarian', 'democratic', or whatever – is likely to be doctrinaire. As our examples in this and the previous chapter show, everything depends on *what sort of interaction* we want to take place: on what sort of business we want to conduct, what our particular purposes are. The style or régime suitable for an army or a ship of war will differ from that suitable for running a railway, a factory or a school. Moreover, it is clear that much depends on the people themselves: their age, or maturity, common sense or natural tendencies. Thus it would be ludicrous to attempt a 'democratic' régime for young children in war-time: first, because such children are not capable of the sort of participation required, and second because the exigencies of war demand rapid obedience to the commands of some clear-cut authority. Equally it would be ludicrous to attempt an 'authoritarian' seminar for intelligent adults: first, because the adults are capable of the relevant participation, and second because anything properly called a 'seminar' could not (almost by definition) be conducted unless the participants actually participated on something like an 'egalitarian' or 'democratic' basis — if it were to be 'authoritarian' it would simply turn into a situation where the professor dictated to the students what they should think and say.

We can see, I think, that little or nothing is gained by doctrinaire preferences ('authoritarian', 'democratic', or whatever). The fact is that very often we do not know what régimes really suit what sorts of people when they conduct various kinds of business. One difficulty is that people may think that a particular régime suits them — usually one in which they are given more direct power in decision-making — but *be wrong*: not only may the régime be inefficient for conducting whatever particular business they are engaged in, but it may also make them feel unhappy, insecure and desperately anxious. Whether it really suits primitive societies to have a democratic government, teenagers to have complete control over their own sexual behaviour, or women to have equal powers of decision-making with their husbands — these are, I think, very open questions which should wait on more psychological and sociological knowledge: though, of course, climates of feeling usually foreclose the questions in different ways at different times.

So far as what suits the particular clientèle is concerned, teachers can only rely on their own common sense and experience, assisted by whatever psychologists and others can tell us. But we can make a good deal more progress by being clear about what suits the business we are conducting. For thereby we become clear about what sorts of decisions need to be made and what sorts of authorities we need to accept and obey: what rules and sanctions are necessary for the business, and what considerations are relevant and irrelevant. Where the nature of our business is fairly obvious, we usually manage to do this: nobody would think of running an army by democratic vote, or trying to solve a mathematical problem by deferring to the *Führer* or the Chief Constable. It is when we are less clear about what we are trying to do that we have doubts about the nature of the authority needed.

If (as I have argued) education is to do with the planning of serious and sustained learning, then we have at least a few obvious points to bear in mind. First, authority must be exercised to ensure that such learning can in fact take place, and to encourage it: and by the same token, we do not require authority to go beyond the purposes of learning. Thus, at least prima facie, the authority would have power and scope to ensure that the pupils did a minimum of work, turned up on time, did not disrupt the teaching, did not interfere with each other in such a way as to prevent each other from learning, and so on. Equally it would *not* have the power or scope to dictate, say, the pupils' dress or hair-styles, unless it could be shown that these directly affected their learning. Of course this is only a very general point: a great deal will depend on *what* is to be learned and — something which follows from that — the *contexts* in which it can best be learned. Both these may be disputed. But at some stage we shall have to commit ourselves (and our pupils) to some sort of content, some set of objectives: and the important thing is to spell these out as clearly as we can. The question of authority can only be answered in that light.

Second, we can ensure that the authority (together with the rules and sanctions that go with it) is *clearly-defined* in its scope and powers, and *properly enforced*. These are, again, obvious points, if much neglected in practice. Everybody in the business — ourselves, the pupils, their parents, and all those connected with the enterprise — need to know just what the rules are, and what sanctions back them up; who can enforce what upon whom, by what methods, and under what circumstances. Unless this is done, those in the business will not know where they are, and if the situation is too vague, the whole existence of any authority may be called into question, with the result that what actually happens is determined by pressure-groups, vociferous individuals, power-seekers, or mere inertia. It is from this sort of chaos, in which the strongest has his way and the weakest goes to the wall, that the entire apparatus of authority, rules, laws, constitutions, sanctions and the rest is supposed to save us: and unless it is defended with remorseless clarity, as well as being revised and overhauled when necessary, chaos is the inevitable result.

Third, we can try (by whatever methods seem appropriate) to show our pupils that the ideal form of authority — for serious learners — really consists of the rules, procedures and standards inherent in what is being learned. Teachers and other educators act as mediators between these standards and the pupils: their job is to bring the pupils, so far as possible, to a state in which they are willing and able to pursue the subjects for their own sake — that is, to obey the demands of truth which each subject incorporates. These demands, as any serious learner well knows, are no less stringent than the orders issued by teachers and other personalized authorities: it is, again, not a matter of escaping from authority and rules altogether, but of accepting the type of authority and rules which are most nearly appropriate to the activity. The whole point of the teacher's authority is to move pupils in this direction.

3 Finally, there is the much more difficult question of the legitimacy of authority in education. Assume that the pupils ought to learn what we want them to learn, that we set up a system of authority in schools which is more or less correct in scope, form, clarity and

enforcement, that we encourage the pupils to question and learn about authority in appropriate ways, and that we succeed in making serious learners of them: even then, it might be asked, by what right do we *compel* them to undergo this process, however desirable it may be? Who are the 'we' that assume the right to enforce this? Do not the pupils themselves have some say in the matter?

The traditional arguments advanced to justify this compulsion include the idea that the desirability of education is alone sufficient; that pupils are too young or too inexperienced to know what their best interests are, and that, being in this state, they can fairly be regarded as under orders (as well as under protection) emanating from their parents, or the state, or some other people to whom authority is delegated — including teachers. In default of lengthy discussion, I must frankly say that these arguments seem entirely unsatisfactory: particularly when applied to (for example) an intelligent fifteen-year-old who does not wish to remain at school but who is legally compelled to do so. At the least, it seems hardly consistent to apply compulsion to such pupils 'in their own best interests' when we do not apply it to others to whom these same arguments might apply; for instance, to the senile, to the very stupid or the hopelessly neurotic, or to backward peoples, and so on.

So far as is possible — and of course with young children it is not possible — we ought surely to adopt the standard liberal practice of negotiation rather than imposition. Roughly speaking, what happens is that the child waives his rights and freedom as an individual in return for protection and nurture: he can at least be construed as giving his parents (society, teachers, etc.) a kind of mandate, rather like that of a colonial occupying power. Only such a basis, as I see it, would justify such imposition: that is, only if we can construe the pupil as voluntarily or contractually putting himself in the hands of the educator, much as a sick person may put himself in the hands of the doctor and surgeon, who may then justifiably command him.

Although this is not, in fact, the legal position, the notion of a contract has important practical applications for teachers. First, it can reasonably be represented to the pupils that, if there *were* a chance for them to make a free contract, they would be well advised to contract for at least some education. Quite a lot of serious learning is required if they are to survive in society, and a good deal more if they are to pull their weight — something which society can legitimately demand — if it is going to protect them and offer them its services. Second, even if they would not freely accept a large part of education, they have nevertheless to adopt some clearly-defined attitude to the system as it stands: either to accept (however grudgingly) or to reject. Teachers and pupils are here in the same boat; it is not the teacher's fault that this compulsion is applied (and teachers should exert whatever political power they have to produce a more rational situation). The teacher can say, in effect, 'This is the law, whether we like it or not, given this – no doubt unreasonable – framework within which we have to operate, what kind of deal can we make with each other?'

The point is that, even when (perhaps particularly when) there is disagreement or resentment, we have to reach some sort of contractual agreement if we are to do any business together. The negotiation which this requires is often lengthy, arduous, and discouraging; but it is better than a state of muddle and conflict in which both sides are, so to speak, trying to play quite different games on the same board. Agreement, however *ad hoc*, must be reached and the important thing is that those concerned should be *clearly committed* to it. Any method which will encourage such clear commitment – for instance, signing one's name to a set of rules – should be adopted (for a discussion of practical methods, see Wilson, 1972b). For without this commitment people (perhaps particularly the young) are apt to regard themselves as outside the game altogether: as able to obey rules when it suits them, and disobey when it does not. But this is a parasitic attitude: social expectations depend, as in the paradigm case of promise-keeping, on a commitment *in advance* to fulfil them (see Rawls, 1972: Hare, 1963; Hart, 1963, Pitkin, 1972).

Many more questions of this kind could, of course, be raised under the general heading 'authority'; but I incline to think that practical answers can only be given by practising teachers – those who actually know the pupils and know what is both politically possible and educationally appropriate in each particular situation. There are many different kinds of schools, having very different relationships with the pupils' parents, local and central government, and the wider community: and pupils vary even more in various dimensions that may be relevant – age, sex, home background, intelligence and so on. It is no part of philosophy to lay down specific rules; nor, in my judgment, have psychology and the social sciences advanced sufficiently to give the teacher much practical guidance. It must be left to his own common sense and imagination.

Nevertheless, there is a sort of general message (as we may call it) which I hope to have got across in the points made above. We are apt to think of authority as a kind of *object* or *force* which we possess in some quantity or other, rather as if we were wielding a stout or fragile stick; then some of us go on to wish that the stick were thicker, and others of us begin to feel guilty about wielding it at all. Even if we ourselves have grown out of these naive ideas, they are certainly present in our pupils' minds. What we have to do is to see clearly, and encourage our pupils to see, that authority is not like that at all: that it is more like the rules of a game, or some other decision-procedure which legitimizes and hence enables whatever business we are trying to do. Too many people still see rules, punishment and authority as restrictive and forbidding only, when in fact they are also enabling: just as keeping to the rules of a language — meaning what we say — may forbid us to use words wrongly, but is the only thing that enables us to communicate.

Given this sort of understanding, we have some hope of being able to sit down together to sort out what games we want to play. The practical difficulties which teachers face derive ultimately from our failure to do this, a failure which, admittedly, is not only or even chiefly the fault of teachers. A great many parties are involved — parents, local authorities, government, the state of the law, and of course the pupils themselves. But it would be a good start if teachers were to be more insistent about reaching some clear agreement with these parties. One would hope (as I tried to argue in chapter 2) that the agreement would entrust teachers with far more authority (and the power to go with it), since the complex business of education seems to demand this sort of set-up; but at least, whatever the agreement, all parties would know where they stood.

Chapter five

Curriculum

Most topics in education have been so inflated with hot air that, like balloons, they have broken any moorings they once had to terra firma. The topic marked by 'curriculum' or 'curricular theory' is an extreme and instructive case of this. Even philosophers, as we shall see, take far too much for granted; but I want to begin by looking at one or two remarks made by non-philosophical 'educational theorists' (if that is the proper description), in order to see just what sorts of things have gone wrong and how they have gone wrong.

Our first concern, as sane and serious students of education, will be to get clear what we are talking about under the heading of 'curriculum' – and what we are *not* talking about, which is of course part of the same enterprise. Some authors' remarks on this seem hard to take seriously; as for instance 'The curriculum consists of the sum of the experiences of learners while they are under the auspices of the school. This simple definition is generally accepted by authorities in the field' (Johnson, 1968, p. 3); or 'It is *everything* that the students and their teachers do. Thus it is twofold in nature, being made up of the activities, the things done, and of the materials with which they are done' (Rugg, 1936, pp. 17–18). It hardly needs saying that if, for instance, a child sitting on a tin-tack, being bullied, day-dreaming, etc., or a student or teacher scratching, breathing and excreting, or chalk, cricket-bats and plasticine are part of what is *meant by the word* 'curriculum', something has dramatically changed in our language, and the compilers of standard dictionaries ought to be told about it.

Naturally when pressed even educational theorists may become slightly anxious about words being stretched to the point not only of vagueness but of unintelligibility. One has the grace to say that 'When curriculum is defined as "the total effort of the school to bring about desired outcomes in school and out-of-school situations" . . . the very breadth may make the definition nonfunctional' (Taba, 1962, p. 9), thought she unfortunately goes on to give a definition not much more intelligible. Other random shots include: 'the curriculum consists of content, teaching methods and purpose', but 'our curriculum includes the pupils getting good jobs in after life' is nonsense — curricula may *have* purposes but do not *consist of* them; 'our curriculum consists of corporal punishment and videotape' is also nonsense — curricula may *use* certain methods but again do not *consist of* them; 'the contrived activity and experience . . . that life, unaided, would not provide', but 'our curriculum contrives that the pupils feel much more and intense stomach-aches than life, unaided, would provide' is absurd. (I am indebted for these examples to Richmond, 1971, p. 10. The former is laid at the door of Professor P. H. Taylor, the latter at that of Professor Frank Musgrove.)

If these examples seem ludicrous, it is not because I have selected them as such. In fact, they are typical. Not much is to be gained by observing the all-too-common case of authors purporting to give 'definitions' — that is, presumably, some adequate account of what a *word means* — when in fact they are doing something quite different, or at least, one hopes that they are; hopes, because if they had seriously been trying to define (translate, paraphrase) the *word* one would have doubts either about their sanity or their grasp of natural language. In fact, it is not clear what they are trying to do. There seems to be some idea of telling us what the curriculum *is* (is made up of?), rather as a physicist might tell us what atoms are made of (rather than what 'atom' means). The confusion here is particularly disastrous for psychology and social science (see Wilson, 1972a, pp. 30ff.). But they are important as showing that we do not know (or perhaps have not agreed) what is to count, and what is not to count, under the title 'curriculum'; and also as showing some of the directions in which (so to speak) the balloon has left the ground — that is, the kind of things these 'definitions' want to cram in. We can already see, I think, two basic ways in which they try to put too much into 'curriculum'. First, too many 'experiences' or 'learning experiences' are included: if a child learns to keep out of the way of the school bully, this has nothing to do with anything one could call a 'curriculum'. Second, too many other things besides 'learning experiences' are included: 'aims', 'purposes', and 'methods', which may be contingently connected with actual curricula but form no part of the sense of 'curriculum'. The former inflation, we may say, expands 'curriculum' to mean in effect 'anything that goes on in schools', or (in a sense) 'the education and upbringing of children'. The latter expands it in a different way, to mean something like 'the curriculum and anything that might be connected with it in our thinking about it', 'curricular theory', or 'the practical and theoretical study of education'.

Why is this important? There are reasons, besides the obvious requirement that we should be clear what we are talking about — though this in itself cuts deep. If I am appointed to run a 'curriculum development project', or apply for grants to study 'the curriculum', or find myself a professor of 'curricular theory', how else am I to know *what* I am supposed to develop, or study, or profess? The reasons have to do with the immense importance of a clear and agreed taxonomy or set of descriptions, making distinctions at the most basic level, for any systematic or (in a broad sense) scientific study: particularly when the study is in its infant stages, as is clearly the case with the study of education. Various practical problems arise: children get bullied, do not learn to read, lack self-confidence, fail to pass an examination in history, and so on. Are any or all or none of these and other issues to be placed under the heading of 'the curriculum'? Or under 'pastoral care', 'pupil—teacher relationships', 'administration', 'the home background', etc.? Are some of them not *educational* problems at all?

Unless we have some clear set of distinctions, some proper set of headings under which particular problems or aspects of problems are agreed to fall, we cannot even start. The objection to the inflation of 'curriculum' is not just 'linguistic' or 'terminological': the point is that this inflation blurs distinctions that we do now have and use – that is, when we are not writing, or bewitched by, textbooks on the topic. Not only that: for those who (unconsciously) expand the sense of 'curriculum' in whatever directions fancy or fashion may lead them do not, of course, totally escape from the pull of the normal meaning of the term. This is an important methodological point, and deserves a little expansion.

Suppose (what I have not yet shown) that we start with a term, 'curriculum', which is fairly tightly tied to *one* aspect of school life only: let us say, to timetabled courses of sustained subject-learning (Latin, mathematics, etc.). We now ask some important question like 'Should moral education be part of, or in, the curriculum?' We have a fairly clear idea of what this question means: it means something like 'Should we have set and regular classroom periods in moral education, *or* does "moral education" need rather to be considered under some other aspect of school life – perhaps under "pastoral care", "the social structure of the school", "extra-curricular activities", or whatever?' (Of course different parts of moral education might come under different aspects.) Now we move on, and 'curriculum' seems to mean something much wider than it used to. I say 'seems', because nobody has taken the task of what it is to mean very seriously. But suppose it is used very widely, to mean roughly 'what happens to pupils in school'. Then *provided that* everyone is clear about this and agrees to it, we simply have a new terminology: instead of asking 'Should moral education in schools be part of the curriculum?', which will now hardly make sense, we have to ask 'Should moral education be done under one aspect of the curriculum – let's call it "timetabled classroom periods" – or under another aspect — let's call it "social experiences" or "pastoral care"?' In other words, because of a change in normal usage we simply have to re-make old distinctions: in particular, we have to find a new term to mark what 'curriculum' in the old sense used to mark.

Now *if* this were done consciously and unanimously, not much harm would ensue: at worst it would be a cumbersome and unnecessary change. But it is not. What in fact happens is that the new use of 'curriculum' covers more ground, but still retains an undertone of its old meaning: that is, a meaning connected with certain kinds of learning, planned by a school, usually able to be set out on paper and attached to a list of 'aims' and 'objectives', and so on. Hence the temptation will be to construe *any* problem on this model: if *anything* is wrong with the school, it will be because 'the curriculum' is somehow faulty. This would indeed be a tautology of some kind, if we really went the whole hog and made the equation 'curriculum' = school experience. But in fact we shall be tempted to seek for solutions by 'curricular' (in the old sense) methods. A similar move has occurred in the fashionable expansion of the terms 'society' and 'social'. If all or nearly all factors and causes are described as 'social', then the word becomes useless, and we shall still, nevertheless, be tempted by the older and saner use of the word to attribute things to (in the older sense) 'social' rather than, say, 'psychological' factors. For instance, in discussions about mental differences between men and women, it is often thought that the possibilities are exhausted by 'genetic' or 'innate' factors, and 'social conditioning' ('social' including parental reactions and expectations in very early childhood). But Freudian-type views which stress the (socially inevitable) interaction between the child's anatomy and his self-image — whether right or wrong — do not fit this dichotomy. So, too, with many other debates; either something is 'innate' (unfashionable) or attributed to 'society', 'the system', etc. (fashionable). No wonder such debates are usually so dull.

Even though 'curriculum' is in some degree a term of art or technical term, then, it is worth getting a little clearer about its normal use. Philosophers of education have not here been of much help (some even seem to think that we don't have to bother to do this: see, for example, Martin, 1970, pp. 1–4): the term is constantly used apparently on the assumption that we are clear already. (See for instance the thirteen index-references in Peters, 1966.) Competent articles about the curriculum (one by Pring and one by Sockett) appear in Peters, 1973; but even here one has the impression that philosophers have played into the hands of educational fashion by allowing far too much to pass unchallenged. Hirst and Peters, for instance, in a chapter entitled, 'The Curriculum', say only 'We shall take the term "curriculum" to be the label for a programme or course of activities which is explicitly organised as the means whereby pupils may attain the desired objectives, whatever these may be' (Hirst and Peters, 1970, p. 60. Cf. Hirst, 1974, p. 2). In the general context, this may perhaps be allowed to pass; for despite 'whatever these may be', the authors tie the notion of education (and hence of the curriculum) fairly tightly to the notion of *sustained learning* and what they call 'cognitive perspective'. But if one took 'whatever these may be' on its own, it will hardly do. For schools might (perhaps often do) have 'objectives' which involve little or no sustained learning: they might rather be attained, or at least thought to be attainable, by quite other methods — encouraging a Spartan attitude by keeping the school dormitories cold or a sense of beauty by placing the school in glorious mountain scenery. Here it would be linguistically absurd to say that cold dormitories or mountains were 'in the curriculum'.

The first condition of application for 'curriculum', then, is that we can use the word only where *learning* is in question. Second, the learning has to be planned or intentionally organized by the educators: unpredictable or chance learning-experiences, however valuable, would not count. Third, and more importantly, the learning has to be to some degree sustained or regular, and (I would say as a sighting shot) serious. 'Sustained or regular' is certainly necessary: an occasional visit to a museum is not part of the curriculum; it begins to qualify as such only if the visits are conceived as part of a sustained and regularized programme of learning. Visiting lecturers, however important, are not part of a curriculum unless similar conditions apply. As a student's supervisor, I may think that he will learn a great deal by (say) having to fend for himself in a foreign country, and I may make plans and arrangements for him to do this — but I do not thereby give him a curriculum.

Most of this is, I think, fairly straightforward. Taking a child's temperature every day may be something on the *timetable*, but cannot be something on the curriculum: no learning is involved, or not enough to count. Timetabled activities like games or PT are borderline cases: borderline, because these can be seen to involve enough learning (like compulsory chess in Russian schools), or not doing so (like the cold dormitories case). Compulsory religious worship would make another interesting and doubtful example. But the three general conditions seem clear enough.

More uncertain is whether we should add some word like 'serious' or 'highly-valued'. One possible reason for doing so is that there are clearly cases of sustained, planned learning which we nevertheless describe normally under the heading of 'extra-curricular activities': for instance, art clubs or debating societies or archaeological groups might meet regularly, and their members learn a lot — and this might be planned or catered for by the educational authorities. Here one might be tempted to say that this has something to do with such clubs not being *compulsory* — but some subject certainly 'in the curriculum' might not be compulsory either. However, the (characteristic) lack of compulsion in extra-curricular activities offers a clue. Many such activities, of course, are not or not primarily activities involving sustained learning, or at least not seen as such, and hence are disqualified as curricular from the start. Those that do involve sustained learning must, I think, be regarded by the authorities as insufficiently important or serious; and this is why they are not included in the curriculum. (For most teachers, we might guess, learning chess is not an essential part of education — chess belongs to the world of clubs, hobbies, games and extra-curricular activities. For Russian teachers, it is seen as essential, and hence part of the curriculum.)

In other words, it seems to be a conceptual rather than just a contingent point that learning activities which constitute 'the curriculum' are those which the educators take most seriously. Failing some reasonable excuse (such as that there is nobody to teach it, or that the pupils are too stupid to learn it), an educator could hardly say 'At this school we think X (English, mathematics, etc.) to be more educationally important than Y (chess, football), but we have Y in the curriculum and X as an extra-curricular activity'; or at least he could of course *say* this, but would have to quote some special reason to make it sound at all reasonable. The learning that goes on under 'curriculum', then, must not only be sustained and regular, but also be taken seriously. As we shall see later, this has important consequences.

Finally, 'curriculum' involves the notion of some *content* which has to be mastered *in stages* or in some kind of order ('programme' is too weak here). 'Course of study', like the (aberrant) usage in 'curriculum vitae', hints at the notion of moving from one stage of learning to another: that is, progressively mastering a particular content or 'form of thought'. At one stage in mathematics, the curriculum includes simple equations, at a later stage quadratic. The (admittedly obscure) notion of a *syllabus* is here very much in place. One could hardly, I think, have a curriculum without some kind of serious syllabus: we must always be able to ask 'What does the course *consist of*?', and the syllabus gives us an answer. This general point seems to tie 'curriculum' closely with certain *kinds* of learning: namely, those that have some sort of definite structure. Thus I may learn to paint largely by watching a master-artist and trying out things by myself, but it would be odd here to talk of a curriculum or a syllabus, there is not enough structure. This too has important consequences.

A good deal of the above could do with some sharpening up and testing by more particular cases; but it is, I hope, sufficient to enable us to move on to some more substantial points. Large-scale and small-scale decisions have to be taken, by governments, local authorities, head teachers and individual teachers, about 'what to do with' various kinds of pupils. I use the wide-open phrase 'what to do with', because it is important here *not* to pre-empt anything by more specific terms. Nearly all current literature in the philosophy of education makes such a pre-emptive move (though quite overtly and honestly: indeed it is essen-tially the move I made in chapter 1 of this book): that is, the move of taking 'education' in a sense tied closely to structured learning, 'cogni-tive perspective', and so on. This sense, as we have seen, fits the normal meaning of 'curriculum' very well. So what we now have is a particular set of concepts, marked by such terms as 'education', 'curriculum', 'serious and sustained learning', 'cognitive perspective', etc., which we may be tempted to take as the starting-point for discussions about what sort of treatment we should give to different kinds of pupils: perhaps 'what sort of curriculum' they should have. My point is that many of the most important decisions *lie behind* this set of concepts, as I shall try to show.

We have seen that 'curriculum' is only properly used for planned, sustained and regular learning, which is taken seriously, which has a distinct and structured content and which proceeds via some kind of stages of learning. Now if we reflect on this — fairly stringent — set of conditions in relation to what may be quite large numbers of pupils (or at any rate *some children*), it immediately becomes apparent that to ask 'What *sort of* curriculum should they have?' may beg many ques-tions. For we might well think that such children should not do very much in the way of serious, sustained, structured learning at all; or we might think them not to be capable of very much. We need rather to ask something like 'How much of "what we do with" these children should be *curricular* at all?' or 'How much do they need a *curriculum* as against, say, pastoral care, hobbies, "interests", and so on?' (as we shall see, it is getting these *other* possibilities sorted out that forms our main task). This would be much the same as asking 'How much *educa-tion* (in the stringent, perhaps monopolized sense discussed above) ought they to have, or how much can they stand? And if not much, what are our other options?'

It has to be remembered that these are very open questions: not, or not only, because they raise complicated philosophical problems about what is worthwhile or valuable, but more obviously because the actual situations of various groups of children in the world can be enormously different. The obviousness of this is masked, not only by a tendency of philosophers and educational theorists to *start off within* the pre-emptive framework of concepts that we have just noted, but also by theoretical debates about whether we can justifiably 'set limits' to chil-dren's ability to learn, whether we can classify some children as 'non-academic', whether 'IQ' is important, etc. Often the position is simpler: children may be starving, terrorized, seriously disturbed, out in the streets throwing bombs at soldiers, and so on. Granted that in many, perhaps most, schools in the UK such situations do not (yet) often apply, nevertheless they do sometimes apply and have to be considered;

and in any case, I take it that philosophers of education should not be so culture-bound as the neglect of such points would suggest.

Nor will it do to assume that these situations are of no concern to the educationalist as such or the school as such. In practice, teachers (parents, local authorities, etc.) are faced with situations of this kind, and other less extreme situations which raise precisely the same problems. Certainly, if we start by talking very generally about 'what to do with' children, it will at *some* stage be worth pointing out that not all the things we 'do with' children would normally count as 'education'; but it is important not to make this move too early. For the problems simply reappear – perhaps in the form of asking how far teachers should act as *teachers* or educators rather than in other roles, or how far the school should see itself as an *educational* institution rather than in other ways.

Some of the dangers here emerge in an interesting, though in my view ultimately misguided, book by one philosopher of education, entitled *Towards a Compulsory Curriculum* (White, 1973. He nowhere tries to establish the *sense* of 'curriculum', although he uses the word hundreds of times). The author's conclusions are, roughly, that there should be a compulsory curriculum for *all* children (except the extreme cases of mental defectiveness and so forth) consisting (again roughly) of the 'forms of thought' outlined by Hirst and Peters (1970, pp. 62ff. Cf. Hirst, 1974). One of the ideas behind this is that all children should be introduced to what *they* may come to see as 'intrinsically valuable' or worth pursuing for its own sake (White, 1973, pp. 17–24) (the children are to be brought up to be 'autonomous', whatever this may mean) (ibid., pp. 21–2); and this means that we must, as Peters elsewhere puts it, get children 'on the inside of' the various forms of thought, mathematics, philosophy, personal knowledge, etc., by compulsion, since otherwise they could not come to appreciate them and hence to choose them for themselves as adults could if they wished to do so (ibid., pp. 25ff.). Other activities, which the child or person can in principle wholly or partly understand without proper engagement in them, can be thought of as more voluntary.

Of course I can do no justice to the argument of such a book here: but it is worth using as an example of what may easily happen if we argue on certain predetermined lines. Many teachers in practical situations – for instance, in schools which serve very 'tough' or depressed areas in the UK, let alone New York or New Guinea, will want to say something like 'but this sort of curriculum doesn't *suit* these particular children', or perhaps (having noticed our earlier points about the sense of 'curriculum') 'it isn't a problem of *curriculum* at all'. I want to argue that this reaction is essentially right, and that the reasons which make it right also offer us a clue to the real distinctions which we need.

The author deals with something like this reaction, but in a significantly tendentious way. He considers the objection that not everybody has the 'innate mental capacity' to manage such a curriculum (ibid., p. 95) because of 'heredity' (ibid., p. 97), and asks 'What kind of evidence would be sufficient to show that a child was constitutionally incapable of following an intellectually demanding curriculum?' (ibid.). He dismisses (no doubt rightly) IQ tests, and also 'poor scholastic performance' (ibid.), and regards the 'innatist claim' as 'pure dogma' (ibid., p. 99). He then admits that the objection may have some practical force 'if it is interpreted as referring to children now (1973) in their last year or so of school', but is unworried because his thesis is concerned 'with children who are being born in 1973 (and later)' (ibid., p. 100).

I describe this as 'significantly tendentious' because he seems unable to imagine any other objection than some kind of 'dogma' about 'innate mental capacity'. I am not at all clear even what 'innate mental capacity' would *mean*; but certainly when a teacher says, for example, 'It's no good teaching this lot much mathematics (history, philosophy, etc.), they won't ever really grasp it or take to it' he would not necessarily be rightly interpreted as adhering to some metaphysic about 'innate mental powers'. But nor would he just mean that, if only the mathematics master took a bit more interest, or the teaching-materials were a bit more effective, or whatever, the children *would* take to mathematics: he means a good deal more than that. Everything turns here on what the author or the teacher might mean by 'constitutionally incapable' or by such phrases as 'they can't (won't) do it'.

Obviously – and this is the author's Aunt Sally – there is one thing they could hardly mean; namely, that there would be some logical contradiction involved in saying that Smith, Jones *et al.* were taking to mathematics. We may press 'can' or 'ability' as gently or as hard as we like: pigs *could* fly, if we mean only that 'a flying pig' is not a contradiction in terms. Maybe, with new technology, new types of child-rearing, and a new social system, children now in the situation of Smith and Jones *would* take to mathematics; but this still allows us to say that the actual Smith and Jones are 'constitutionally incapable' of it. They cannot concentrate, sit still and learn, acquire enough interest, grasp the rather complicated concepts and so on, and their inability here seems, at least, to have something to do with the sort of children they (already) are – dull, day-dreaming, frightened, stupid or whatever. As things are, they cannot do it: in no different way from the way in which, as things are, not every child can become a concert pianist or a chess master. As things might be – well, perhaps in the year AD 2000 we find ways of stimulating the brain cells so that every child can rival Schnabel or Fischer. But that is not what, in most contexts, we normally mean by 'can'.

It is, in fact, clear enough that teachers are up against something pretty basic here (though not necessarily to be construed as something 'innate': there is an important middle ground between the 'innate' and the more obvious area of teaching methods, 'socialization', having more books in the home, and so on. This is the same mistake that we noticed earlier, see p. 65.) Often we do not *know why* it is correct to say that certain children cannot do things, though we may give descriptions in the target-area — usually something to do with lack of parental care, 'achievement motivation', language-use and so on. There are also plenty of surprising cases: that is, cases of children who turn out to be able to do things when we thought they could not, and unable when we would have expected them to have been able. In our present state of ignorance, which is likely to endure for some time, we have to take the facts as they are: they speak much more strongly than, and differently from, the way in which the author allows them to.

This has all the more force, surely, when we remember that most of what teachers have to take as 'given' with regard to their children, and that blocks progress, is often better described under 'motivation' or 'interest' than under 'ability'. There are difficult, perhaps insoluble, problems involved in severing these two — which is why the most natural thing to say is often something like 'Well, I don't know whether at bottom it's that the children can't or that they don't want to, but anyway I'm quite sure they *won't* in fact do such-and-such'. We can know this, as many teachers perfectly well know it, without being able to identify the factors involved, and certainly without holding some theory about them. This sort of knowledge and belief is already available to anyone who knows the child concerned reasonably well: as when parents say 'He's not the studying type'. Of course such judgments may be wrong; but certainly not always, and in any case my point is that there is something to judge here.

The merits of this author's curriculum, or any other curriculum, must obviously depend not only on some very 'pure' concept of ability but also on these factors, which we ineptly describe under headings like 'motivation', 'interest' and so on. Other descriptions might be better. We may talk of 'seriousness', 'powers of concentration', 'application', or with some psychologists of the 'super-ego', 'deferred gratification', and 'maturity'. The pupils must have enough of these if they are to be introduced to or initiated into various subjects or 'forms of thought' in any serious sense: of course it is possible to get them to go through the motions (though even that would be barely possible with many children); but sufficient initiation to enable them to get the feel of the subjects, so that (as the author wants) they can weigh their value in making their choices about what to pursue, demands a high degree of 'seriousness', 'ability and willingness to concentrate', or however we describe it.

This is, in part, why I wanted to defend the teacher's natural remark that such-and-such 'doesn't *suit*' the children. 'Suit' seems in order here because it draws attention to whatever we mean when we talk of a child's 'natural' inclination, his 'bent', the *sort* of pursuits he is likely to follow. Is he imaginative? Does he like precision and getting things right? How interested is he in learning new things generally? Does he search for it in books or elsewhere? What aspects of the world have glamour for him? What does he want to be like? These are questions to which we give answers largely based on experience of the child and other children, and our own ability ('insight', if you like). But these are the questions on which we have to base our answers about 'what to do with' various children.

I should maintain that the question of what suits, or is best for, a person can only be coherently answered in terms of his own and other people's happiness (roughly, on the grounds that this criterion delimits what is to count as a good reason for action) (cf. Quinton, 1973, pp. 366ff. and Taylor in Ryan, 1973, pp. 165ff.); but whether this is helpful or not, it needs to be made clear that the notion of 'suiting' need not involve us in a number of theses with which it is commonly associated. First, it does not all imply that the child, or even the adult, is the best judge of what suits him. There is a common notion (White, 1973, pp. 18ff.) that individuals can be said in some *general* way to be in a better position to know their own needs than other people are; but, as I have pointed out elsewhere (Wilson, 1973, pp. 107ff.), a man can be mistaken even about what he wants or enjoys, let alone about what is good for him. Much depends on his capacity for honest and careful self-inspection: not only self-deception but also forgetfulness, carelessness and other factors may operate against him. The best judge is a wise man who knows the person intimately and loves him. Second, we may also grant that *part* of what may suit a person – or perhaps may to a degree suit or be good for every person – consists of learning things: even of learning quite difficult and daunting things, from which men may gain little pleasure and in which they may have little natural interest. There are other obvious reasons for this besides the desirability (if this indeed be granted) of the 'autonomous choice' which a person can make when he has been introduced to activities which he might otherwise have neglected. It is clearly desirable on many grounds, social as well as (in a stricter sense) educational, that children should – putting it very roughly – be encouraged and perhaps compelled to learn as much as they can reasonably be said to stand; and it may even be that certain kinds of learning-content (the 'forms of thought') can be shown to be especially valuable.

But none of this touches the substantive questions, which arise in the general form of '*In so far as* a "curriculum" (sustained and structured learning) does not suit certain children (or does not best serve their interests, or however we choose to deploy some such criterion), what *other* modes of treatment can we consider?' Now of course the practical answers to particular questions, asked of specific children in specific situations, will depend on much more than philosophy. But perhaps the philosopher can be of some help in offering a few simple categories, within which these practical questions can be considered. I will only take a few steps in this direction, because obviously this is an enormous task which can only properly be accomplished by sustained interdisciplinary research. What follows is, if you like, just common sense ('phenomenological description', if you want a grand term for it).

It seems to me that, in terms of the difficulties and obstacles we have been talking about (lack of concentration, or 'seriousness', or whatever we may say), we may construct a kind of simple hierarchy as follows:

1 Least demanding, there is the situation where the children do not *do* things in any serious sense at all *we* do things *to* them. We hug them, give them sweets, listen to them, smile at them and so on, or – a rather thin kind of 'doing' – the children breathe, eat, sleep, daydream, walk about, perhaps vaguely watch television. No *learning* is involved here at all.

2 More demanding are situations in which children do things in a stronger sense: that is, they engage in what may fairly be called 'activities' which have some kind of structure, may involve taking means to ends, thinking, concentrating, achieving, appreciating, organizing or in general *confronting* the world. They may play games, keep pets, enjoy music, and so forth. Here, though there may be some learning involved, the activities are not activities *of* learning. We do not usually play games *in order to* learn, and in fact we may not actually learn much or anything when we play. Keeping pets is not an activity of learning, and to like keeping pets is not to like learning.

3 More demanding still are situations which are avowedly learning situations. These extend beyond the normal sense of 'curriculum', as we have seen earlier. One may learn to play chess as a hobby, learn about foreign countries when visiting them, learn the guitar, and so on. There are of course plenty of borderline cases between this category and (2) above, but the basic distinction is clear enough – it is a distinction between the points or purposes of the two types. In (2), a person tries to keep a pet or play football; in (3), he tries to *learn* about how to keep pets or how to play football.

4 Most demanding of all are learning situations which are still further removed from what we may call 'natural' interests than the examples

of learning situations in (3). People may in some sense 'naturally' take to learning games, musical instruments, boat building, or how to win friends and influence people: these connect, though often in obscure ways, with standard and immediate interests which are often readily identifiable. This is not true, I think, of (for example) higher mathematics or physics, serious philosophy, the study of Anglo-Saxon literature, or the complexities of the Athenian tribute lists during the Peloponnesian War. It is true, however (or more true, if such a phrase be allowed), of *some* of the things which the orthodox literature describes, badly, as 'forms of thought'; for instance, the appreciation of the arts, involvement in religion, and some aspects of morality and 'personal knowledge' (Hirst and Peters, 1970, pp. 62ff.). This I take to be the concealed truth behind common remarks to the effect that some activities are more 'abstract', 'intellectual' or 'highbrow' than others (and, as the last word shows, this notion has *some* application to the appreciation of the arts).

If I had to specify what this is a hierarchy *of*, I should have to say something like this: it is ordered in relation to the degree that an average person has to put *himself* — that is, his 'natural' desires and impulses and interests — in the background, in the interests of his subject-matter. What is 'demanding' about the more sophisticated items in the hierarchy is that the person has to pay more and more attention to realities *outside* himself, and submit himself to more and more discipline; that is, in so far as he has not yet learned to invest emotionally in these more sophisticated items. Of course some people, and a few children, invest in them at an early stage; but I am claiming, empirically, that this is rare.

It may also be possible to make some conceptual claim here. One might argue that a full explication of the notions in each item would carry with it the notion of increased psychological demand. Thus in (1) there are no demands at all; in (2), since the person is doing something, he must be attending to the real world in some degree — otherwise he could hardly be described as doing *that*. In (3), by definition a situation of learning, he has to suppress his natural desires to operate by direct physical action on the world, and attend to it still more as an object of reflection. He has to tolerate doubt, acquire new concepts, and so forth. And in (4) I have, admittedly in a rather cavalier way, tried to single out those particular types of learning which seem to me extreme cases of this.

Of course all this is sketchy; but rather than waste the reader's time by further elaboration or defence, I would like to suggest that this is the *sort* of categorization or set of distinctions which we need to work on for most practical purposes. We have to start, as we have seen, much further back than what is enshrined by 'curriculum', and begin to think in a systematic way about 'what to do' with the children we are faced with. Naturally this connects, in practice, with what powers we have as teachers, parents, etc., but the important question of what powers teachers and others *ought* to have will itself turn on what we think desirable for children. But in any case we have to ask questions like 'Given whatever powers we now have, what modes of treatment suit these children?' If this question were faced squarely, it might be that we should come up with very different sets of answers. But it cannot be faced squarely under the heading of 'curriculum'.

Many children (even in the UK, and certainly throughout the world), I would guess, are not suited by any very sophisticated curriculum, or even perhaps by anything one could seriously call a 'curriculum' at all. Of course this *is* just a guess; but certainly it will be true of some children. Their particular needs are often more basic; to be socially viable, to be able to love, and to be given the chance to pursue whatever genuine and worthwhile interests they *do* happen to pick up from us. This is not, of course, an argument for not taking however much 'curriculum' we think suitable for them with the utmost seriousness (rather than watering it down so that it ceases to be serious learning at all). It is, rather, an argument for making much sharper distinctions here. If a child looks like being, or can be encouraged to be, genuinely interested in *literature* or *history*, then we thank our lucky stars and set him seriously to work; if he is not, we try something else, or admit that his more basic needs have been so ill-met that serious learning is not for him – and then we must try to cater for these needs much more directly. Nothing is gained by diluting literature into trashy books 'relevant to the modern world', or diluting history into 'environmental studies'; that way we lose on both counts. If they need love or discipline, then we must give them love and discipline in as straightforward a way as possible: not via 'relevance' or other desperate attempts to engage their interest. And if they can manage to meet the demands of serious learning, we must keep the demands serious.

Issues of this kind can, as I have said, only be settled by those who *know* the particular children concerned (see also chapter 2, pp. 26ff.), not by politicians, local authorities, or 'curriculum theorists'. Common sense, assisted by some such set of categories as I have suggested, is here our chief tool. At the sophisticated level, where it may be profitable to consider the content of the curriculum, 'forms of thought', etc., more closely, other problems arise: with these I have not here been concerned. It is in this much more basic area that work needs to be done. Until then, it is more important that teachers should keep their heads, and use them, than that they should pay much attention to 'curricular theory'.

This apparently cavalier dismissal of 'curricular theory' does not at all imply that there is no serious intellectual work to be done here. On the contrary, my case is that the problems are so methodologically complex that most existing work is premature and superficial. In particular, as soon as we raise natural questions beginning 'What sorts of things should children . . . ?', it becomes obvious that we shall have enormous problems concerning the *criteria of differentiation* for these 'things' — even if they are conceived wholly within the category of 'learning', 'curriculum', or 'forms of thought'. What tends to happen in 'curricular theory' is that various theorists (Bloom and Hirst are two obvious examples. See Bloom, 1964; cf. Wilson, 1972a, pp. 104ff.; Hirst and Peters, 1970, pp. 62ff.; Hirst, 1974) impose their own particular criteria of differentiation, which are then either slavishly followed or bitterly opposed by those whose criteria are different. The only process that can be of real practical value to teachers and of real intellectual value in itself, would be the development of an increasingly clear and sophisticated taxonomic or phenomenological analysis of these 'things' (into which some existing work on 'curriculum' might usefully fit). We shall look at these and some other relevant points in the next chapter.

Chapter six

Subjects

'Teaching one's own subject(s)' obviously stands for something which is of immediate practical concern to all teachers: not only in secondary schools, where teachers are usually professionally identified by their subject, but also in other cases. Even primary school teachers who run an 'open-ended, child-centred, integrated day' with 'team teaching' (or whatever the appropriate jargon is) must presumably recognize that their children learn some sorts of things at some times, and other sorts at other times; and this is really all we need for *some* concept of a 'subject'. But how *are* we to conceive of 'subjects'? And can anything general be said about the 'aims' of teaching them, or about how we could most sensibly make some kind of chart or categorization of them, or about which are worth learning?

Clearly there are a large number of very different questions here, even without going into any questions about *methods* of teaching subjects (questions obviously premature if we are not yet sure how to conceive of subjects and their 'aims' — which is what makes most of what is called 'method work' in teacher-training so dubious). Traditionally schools and other educational institutions have taken much of their lead from the universities; and I shall want eventually to argue that there are good reasons for this. But recently there have been changes. It is not just that schools are liable to 'social' or 'instrumental' pressures from government, industry, or other utilitarian forces: that is nothing new. Perhaps the important difference is that schools have become more free to make up their own minds (or have them made up for them by 'educationalists'). All sorts of ideas and fashions are generated, often under the heading 'curriculum development' (see chapter 5), which either take root or wither, and which bear no necessary relation either to academic notions of 'subjects' (as represented at reputable universities, for instance) or to the demands of industry or technology.

Whilst in some respects this may be seen as a welcome situation, it is also obviously a dangerous one. For in so far as any idea put into practice does not have to meet clear and easily testable demands — getting pupils into a university, or turning out enough trained surgeons — there is no clear 'pay-off' which might otherwise save us from muddle or fantasy: nobody goes bankrupt or dies on the operating table. In such a situation, the only thing that can defend us is an unusually hard-headed and sophisticated attempt to be clear and precise in what we say and think. Unfortunately the particular area in question, 'subjects', happens to be a peculiarly difficult one, as we shall see: partly for lack of clear linguistic conventions. I cannot even try to do more here than open up some of the problems that seem important.

We might fairly start where most teachers start: that is, with their own particular subject (X). In training, they are very properly made to become more conscious of this subject: not only in regard to various methods or techniques of teaching it, but in regard to its nature or value. Thus there will be a lot of talk about the 'aims' or 'objectives' of teaching X (history, mathematics, English, etc.). We need a distinction here between (a) what we can call 'external aims' — roughly, various desirable spin-offs one might get from learning X (for example, learning history may diminish race prejudice, learning English may improve self-confidence); (b) 'internal aims' — what sorts of things a person is supposed to know and understand by learning X in itself. 'Internal aims' is not a very good description. One might fairly say 'In teaching maths we aim to get pupils to grasp the principles of multiplication, quadratic equations, etc.', for 'aim' is a loose sort of word (*pace* Peters, 1973, pp. 12ff., cf. pp. 30ff.); but (b) is really an expanded answer to the question 'What *is it to* teach X?' or 'What *constitutes* X as a subject?'

It seems sensible to start with (b) the 'internal aims'. No doubt it is nice if teaching X, Y and Z diminishes race prejudice, makes better citizens, improves social mobility and self-confidence, encourages 'creativity' (whatever that is), and so on; and certainly it is fashionable to put such aims down on lists supposed to 'justify' various subjects. But we do not know whether teaching X, Y and Z actually does produce these desirable results; nor could we possibly find out until we *first* reached some agreement about what it *was to* teach X, Y and Z. There is some danger that whatever values may exist in the 'internal aims' will be forgotten about in a too-hasty desire to make all our pupils happy and good in some general way quite independent of particular subjects.

An obvious way of dealing with the question 'What is it to teach X?' is to look at the word 'X' and see what would normally count as a case of X and what would not. For instance, giving pupils a grasp of French grammar is plainly part of what is meant by 'teaching French'; giving them a taste for Burgundy rather than beer, or a knowledge of French geography, plainly is not. A lot of cases will be clearly seen as falling inside or outside the concept by this technique; and it is hard to think of any other technique which will enable us to make the distinctions we need.

We need the distinctions, because otherwise we cannot make sensible judgments about what to teach various types of pupils at various times; without the distinctions we cannot know what we are judging *between*. For instance: imagine one course which teaches classics in the old way (Latin and Greek grammar, etc.), and another course which gives the pupils some idea of Roman society and ancient Greek art. Now these are obviously different: a difference masked by calling them both 'classics'. The first course would normally count as 'teaching Latin'; the second is certainly not teaching *Latin*, and it is odd even to call it teaching *classics* ('classics' only makes sense in reference to classical languages and literature). We might call it 'Roman and Greek culture' or 'ancient sociology' or something. Then when (only when) we are clear what the differences actually are, we can start thinking about how far this or that course would benefit this or that group of pupils.

Concentrating on the title-words ('teaching Latin', etc.) is just a way of getting at the distinctions we need. But, as this example shows, the technique has difficulties or perhaps limits. For to some degree these words are terms of art, no longer in 'normal usage': made so just by being used as subject-titles in a semi-technical field (education). Lessons *are*, perhaps regrettably, called (say) 'French lessons' even if the pupils do not do anything in them that could seriously be described as learning French. 'English' is worse still. So we have to move, as always in philosophy but with particular care here, back and forth from the title-words to what actually goes on.

We might anticipate the most difficulty with title-words or phrases which entitle what look like 'looser' subjects — perhaps 'social studies' or 'liberal studies' or 'RE'. But actually difficulties in answering our question 'What is it to teach X?' — that is, to teach X *rather than Y* — crop up even in apparently 'tight' subjects. For instance, one might think that mathematics at least was clear-cut: either something is a case of learning this or it is not. Not a bit of it: suppose I am teaching children some very basic notions about space and time and volume or about class-inclusion ('set theory') or simple logic; are any of these specifically and peculiarly *mathematical*? Don't they (one might say) come into practically all subjects and practically all thinking — at least into a good many kinds of thinking which are not specific to mathematics?

Or take 'teaching English'. When very young children pick up the English language from their parents, the parents would not be said to be 'teaching English'. Are the children 'learning English'? Well, we have to say 'yes' to that, but with a little unease. 'English' sounds a bit odd here, because we normally use it (in the context of our present discussion)

79

as a *subject*-title, and we feel that the children are not exactly learning a subject, they are just learning to talk. So are we going to reserve 'English' as a subject-title for some activity which is (as it were) rather grander and more specialized than just learning to talk and understand – the study of grammar and syntax and literature and so on? Clearly *in a sense* 'English' comes into most other subjects, since most other subjects demand the use of English words and the understanding of them.

It is important here *not* to make the move of saying 'There, you see, really every subject overlaps with every other subject, the "barriers" between subjects are "artificial".' Saying this is just throwing in the towel. For part of the problem is to decide when to count some apparent difference as 'artificial'. For instance, we have three title-words, 'arithmetic', 'algebra', 'geometry'. Now some mathematicians will tell you that to some extent these three subject-titles cover 'the same ground': that is, perhaps, it is the same basic mathematical principles that are learned in all three. For that reason they might want to call the differences 'artificial', and in practice combine the three titles under one heading, perhaps 'Basic mathematics'. Or again, and more simply, if we have one course called 'history' which consists of the study of Elizabethan England, and another course called, say, 'The background to Shakespeare', which also consists of the study of Elizabethan England, but which appears under the title 'English literature', we shall suspect some artificiality – although, of course, it may be that the second course concentrates only on those historical facts which are directly relevant to Shakespeare or his plays; and now this is *some* sort of difference, which we should have to elucidate and argue about.

We are arguing in such cases about what criteria of similarity and differentiation to use. Now the first thing to be said in such a situation is that we are not compelled to use only *one* such criterion; and since criteria are used for particular purposes (and not just for taxonomic fun) we shall need to apply *all* the criteria which look as if they might be important and try to marry up the differences, so enforced, with our own various purposes and values. I mean something like this: we start, say, with the title-words 'arithmetic', 'algebra', 'geometry', then, after reflection and a good deal of research, we might want to say:

1 By the criterion of (roughly) logical similarity of the principles learned, these three titles cover the same ground.
2 By the criterion of the symbols or medium of expression used, they cover different ground (one uses numbers, another Xs and Ys, and another lines and shapes).
3 By the criterion of (roughly) what is useful to know for particular social purposes (counting change, etc.), they cover different ground.

4 By the criterion of what is in some sense intrinsically attractive to pupils, they cover different ground (maybe 'visual' types of pupils naturally take to geometry, 'verbal' types to algebra, etc.).

And so on: these are only *some* of the criteria we might want to use.

Now all this is immensely complicated and large-scale; but there does not seem to be any other way of going about it. If we do not try to make our criteria conscious, and to apply them in detail to existing and possible subjects, we get driven in an unconscious way by the tacit pressure of particular purposes or feelings. For instance, we may be driven by criteria like 'what the pupils enjoy', 'what is relevant to the modern world' (whatever that means), and so on. These *may* be important criteria; but we cannot know how important except by comparison with other criteria. So we have to try and list these. In this generalized form, the task looks daunting; but if carried out piecemeal, subject by subject, it should not be beyond our powers.

We have a fair start, so far as *one* criterion goes, from Paul Hirst's work on 'forms of thought', too familiar, I hope, to need explanation (Hirst and Peters, 1970, Hirst, 1974. I have a good many reservations about these works, but they are not directly relevant here). That is, we can ask in each case some question such as 'What's the *logic* of whatever is being learned here? What logical types of propositions (evidence, verification, "tests for truth", etc.) are involved?' It is tempting to make this *the* criterion, on purist grounds: what makes a game 'the same' or 'different', we might think, has nothing to do with what symbols it uses, or what use it is, or whether people like it — it is a matter of whether the *rules* are the same or different, a matter of its internal logic. This is *an* important point, relevant, surely, in so far as we are concerned with pupils coming to value a conceptual domain 'for its own sake', to speak roughly. Someone who really likes history as a discipline or 'form of thought' (as against having a penchant for the Middle Ages, or needing to know the background facts of the Arab-Israeli conflict because he works in the Foreign Office) must — and this is a point of logic — like the enterprise of historical enquiry in general. But just because this is a point of logic, we do not have to attribute any particular weight to it in our scale of values of purposes (though there may be other arguments for doing so).

At the other end of the scale, so to speak, our thinking may be monopolized by the criterion of what is (or is thought to be) 'interesting' or 'relevant' to the pupils or students. Characteristically this criterion has been applied by a (largely tacit) extension of traditional subjects; but a person totally dedicated to it could, I take it, always put up some kind of argument, however absurd it might sound to us. Suppose (as is not wholly ludicrous, in an age when even universities run four-year courses in Black Studies, Antarctic Culture and Aeroplane Administration) that someone invented a subject called 'A-K', in which pupils began by learning about aardvarks and abacuses and ended with *kyrie eleison*; even most modern educationalists would think it odd. But the reason even for this is not immediately clear; after all, we accept that a student might just happen to be interested in black people, or the Antarctic, or in being an air hostess. 'But in these cases there is at least some sort of focus, some kind of string that holds them together.' 'Yes, but the A-K volumes of an encyclopaedia hold "A-K" together, and some children might just be interested in amassing knowledge in this way.' We can now make a standard philosophical move and say, 'All right, then, what about "Tuesday Studies" in which pupils learn only about whatever happens to have occurred on Tuesdays?' But now, either we cannot conceive of *any* human interest or focus which would make this intelligible, in which case 'Tuesday Studies' is a mere philosophical example — I mean that, *if* it ever existed this would itself show that it represented an interest or focus; or else we stretch our brains and think of one (Tuesday is a holy day, or the day when workers recover from a black Monday, or whatever).

We feel here two temptations. One is to say something like 'Well, pupils just ought not to be educated in this kind of way, picking up knowledge structured only by the (in a sense arbitrary) order of letters in the alphabet, or only by some curious concern that a particular culture may have with Tuesdays. There just are certain important subjects — even if we have not got the titles properly distinguished and organized — and pupils should be taught them, or at least some of them: or anyway, we should keep to these subjects as a basis.' But the trouble with this is that we cannot be sure that our existing subjects are a *rational* basis: the ancient Babylonians no doubt had astrology on the timetable. Nor, in my judgment, are there overwhelmingly persuasive arguments (Peters, 1966, pp. 157ff., cf. Downie, 1974, chapters 2–4) for taking some subjects or 'worthwhile activities' as 'important' or 'worthwhile' in this *a priori* way — that is, independently of the different kinds of pupils who learn them (these arguments are complicated and I cannot go into them here; see however p. 113). The other temptation is to say 'There are no really important distinctions except those stemming from the child's interests, or what is "relevant to modern society"; so we should allow subjects to come and go according to people's interests, or perhaps drop the whole idea of a subject altogether.' And the trouble with this is, not only that perhaps there *are* important distinctions of other kinds, but also that we have to arrange schools and timetables on *some* sort of basis and by some kind of distinctions, even if we call them 'study areas', 'foci of interest', etc.

This perhaps reinforces what we saw earlier about the importance of close linguistic attention to the concepts marked by subject-titles. For clearly, unless we have already gone overboard for one preferred criterion, we shall *first* need to have a clear account of *what is being learned* under a particular title: only then can we begin to apply various criteria of the value or suitability of what is being learned. Thus there exist people who would wipe all distinctions and subject-titles off the map, replacing them all by the single word 'environment' or 'man'. But then the initial problems reappear — very obviously, as soon as anyone seriously starts to plan, teach, or in any adequate way examine work on 'environment', he will need to be clear about what *sorts* of things are supposed to go on under this heading. To deny the necessity of this is already to have opted for the single criterion of 'relevance' or 'interest'. Even then, this approach may not be coherent: distinctions will, in practice, be made in work done under the heading of 'environment' — how could they not be? — however little attention may be paid to them.

There are, of course, a good many other criteria (besides those mentioned) which operate in practice. Commonly they are used both to define the subject and, by some sort of implication, to endorse its value. For instance, the traditional teaching in the UK of the subject variously called 'RE', or 'RI', 'religious education', etc., clearly relies on some (admittedly imprecise) idea of 'transmitting a Christian (religious, cultural) heritage'. It is thought, not absurdly, that pupils in the UK should have some understanding of, if not belief in, the Christian institutions and literature that have been historically important to their country — the Church, the Bible, and so forth. This idea both determines what the subject of 'RE' *is* — what it consists of — and, by this determination, implies that this is what the subject *ought* to be. Various attacks may then be made: philosophers will say (Wilson, 1971, chapter 1), 'But that will not do as a proper definition of "religious education" ', or educationalists will become aware of substantial numbers of immigrants for whom this is *not* a 'heritage', or there may be pressure to drop the traditional approach in favour of discussion about 'ultimate values' (or whatever). These are the kinds of practical pushes and pulls to which subjects are liable.

I do not see much chance of getting out of this miasmic situation without the kind of taxonomic operation mentioned earlier. Obviously teachers by themselves could not manage this. It seems to be primarily a task for philosophers, drawing upon whatever empirical knowledge is both relevant and well-established (not much, in my judgment) (Wilson, 1975, chapters 2 and 3). But meanwhile teachers have to adopt some sort of attitude; and it may be possible, even before this operation, for us to discern the outlines of a sensible general approach: even though, of course, much will always depend on the particular situation (the sort of children we are dealing with, the availability of teachers, etc.). First of all, our difficulties may be palliated by separating off objectives which do not necessarily involve the pursuit of subjects in their own right or for their own sake. By this I mean simply that, in so far as we have to be concerned with utilitarian or 'social' requirements, these can be dealt with on their own without too much conceptual difficulty. For they are both obvious and often, as it were, *ad hoc*, if a particular society at a particular time desperately needs more soldiers or sheet-metal workers, or if its children have to learn to watch out for sabre-tooth tigers or fast cars, this demand will usually be fairly clear and fairly easily met by specific forms of training. The kinds of difficulties we have been looking at arise, rather, when we start thinking in a more general way about what is 'worthwhile' for children to learn, or what subjects are 'important', irrespective of particular social demands or contexts.

The sort of approach I have in mind may be clarified by considering the notion of specialization. Those who defend this notion − as against the idea that it is somehow shocking if pupils do not know something of a fair number of subjects, 'disciplines', 'forms of thought' or whatever (A. D. C. Peterson is a leading proponent of this idea: see Yudkin, 1969) − rightly rely on the importance of pupils acquiring a genuine enthusiasm for *something* and being encouraged to pursue it. Mary Warnock, for instance, asks for 'serious consideration of the merits of specialization for everyone' (including the 'non-academic') (in Peters, 1973, p. 121) on something like these grounds − to develop the imagination, avoid boredom, etc. But a problem immediately arises about the concept itself: what is to *count as* 'specializing'? If a pupil does nothing but languages? Nothing but classical languages? Nothing but Greek? Nothing but Homeric Greek? Would not somebody who devoted very earnest attention solely to what happened on Tuesdays count as specializing? Could not one specialize in the outlines of world history, rather than in certain aspects of the Italian Renaissance? The notion of specialization itself is context-dependent − that is, dependent on current subjects, 'disciplines', etc. − and is hence equally vulnerable and uncertain.

This throws us back to the important idea which underlies it, that of encouraging pupils to be keen, enthusiastic or 'serious' (see Peters, 1966, pp. 162ff.) about *anything*. Such an idea is very different from the picture of meeting pupils' particular current interests in an *ad hoc* sort of way, of just 'keeping them interested'; we are concerned here with some abiding and genuine interest in some subject, topic, or type of study for its own sake. If, as some philosophers (ibid., pp. 157ff.) think (but I do not), there are overwhelming reasons for supposing that some already-defined subjects or disciplines − what Peters calls 'curriculum activities' (ibid.) − *must* be the proper objects of this seriousness or abiding interest, so much the better; this may at least give us a kind of touchstone for seriousness, or enable us to predict what serious pupils will want to be serious about. But in any case, seriousness gives us an important criterion to hang on to − I think, from a strictly educational point of view, by far the most important.

There is, I think, some conceptual connection between being a serious learner and anything that we could plausibly call a 'subject'. Just as anything properly to be described as a 'curriculum' (see chapter 5, pp. 66ff.) involves serious and structured learning, so any 'subject' involves a fairly high degree of application, concentration, and sophistication on the part of the student. Studying a subject is some way removed from being more or less vaguely interested in some topic or part of one's experience, and very far removed from what is usually meant by 'learning from experience': that is, picking up some facts, skills or attitudes in an *ad hoc*, unstructured sort of way. Granted that such things as music or painting may be subjects, nevertheless subjects characteristically demand some *withdrawal* from immediate experience, some adequate attempt to step back and put the subject-matter under a microscope, as it were. There is a fairly sharp contrast between *studying* some part of the environment and just *interacting* with it. 'Learning-experiences' in mountain-climbing, on board ship or on many school outings, are not normally described as the study of subjects: a person who seriously studies sailing does something different from one who partakes of the experience, however beneficial, of helping to crew a sailing-ship across the Atlantic. And to study music or painting – to relate to them as *subjects* – is something more than, or at any rate different from, the exercise or development of natural artistic talent.

This is not to deny either that, as we saw in the last chapter, many pupils may not be capable of much serious learning at all, or that there are other things that one can seriously learn besides subjects – for instance, how to trust people or to be kind, to love or to keep one's temper. But we have to keep this particular kind of learning, marked by the word 'subjects', clearly in mind: not only to put whatever value we give it into proper practice, but also to be able to compare that value with the value of other learning. If we fail to do this, both are likely to suffer. First, we water down the traditional or clearly-established subjects until they become mere topics or foci of interest, where not much serious learning of any kind goes on: masking what we have done by retaining the traditional subject-titles. Second, we entertain the vague hope that if we liberalize the tradition in this way the pupils will learn other things effectively – 'creativity', 'social concern', 'self-confidence' and so on, and this prevents our tackling this other, non-subject, learning in any direct and adequately forceful way – we just hope, or pretend, that pupils will learn to be kind, to love, to trust and so on simply by *not* having to learn academic subjects in the orthodox way.

Our position, then, is something like this; we accept that, at least for certain pupils at certain times, subject-learning is important. But we find great difficulty in determining the criteria by which we are to demarcate subjects; and, clearly connected with this, a difficulty about deciding which ones to put before our pupils. How can the notion of seriousness help us here? There are, of course, some arguments of a general or conceptual kind to be noted: from the notion of 'being serious' about anything, or more specifically about *learning* things (subjects), various points may be thought to follow. Thus one line of argument would concentrate on the psychological aspects of seriousness, and stress the importance (for any pupil) of 'ego-strength', the ability to love, and hence of any 'subjects' or procedures which might improve our pupils' psychic resources in general: perhaps some kind of psychological study, or the study of literature, or perhaps procedures which might better come under such headings as 'pastoral care', 'group therapy', etc. (cf. Wilson, 1972b, part 4). Another line involves pointing, in a much more practical way, to what seem to be requirements for almost *any* sort of learning or study. These may be of various kinds: on the one hand, we can talk of 'basic skills', of which literacy seems the most obvious, and on the other we can talk of various general abilities — 'straight thinking', 'conceptual competence', etc. — which are generally distinguishable from the 'psychological aspects' mentioned in the former line of argument by being (roughly) more obviously connected with *intellectual* powers.

These lines of thought are worth mentioning for a strictly practical reason: that, in so far as they have force (and obviously they have such force in general, whatever we may think about some of the details), they need urgent attention in schools. A child who is too 'disturbed' or 'withdrawn' or for whatever reason unable or unwilling to concentrate or be interested in anything in the outside world, in any serious way, needs whatever techniques and educational methods we can bring to bear on him *rather than* any 'subjects'. Similarly a child who cannot read fluently enough to profit from books, or who cannot express himself properly both orally and on paper, seems to need education in these 'basic skills' as a priority. But the trouble with such points is that either they are so obvious as to be hardly worth stating, or they are systematically disputable. Of course everyone will agree that 'being able to concentrate', 'fluent reading', etc., are *in general among* desirable aims for pupils. But, first, this is not of much help in relation to what is desirable for a particular child at a particular point in time — here the points are too general; and second, there are no doubt other desiderata with which they may come into conflict — and here, if we are not careful, we shall find ourselves constructing high-level theories or 'doctrines of man', from which it would follow that (for instance) fluent reading is somehow more 'important' or 'valuable' than, say, fluent computation or the skilled use of tools.

I do not say that conceptual or high-level arguments of this and other kinds are without force; and certainly it is too strong, or rather too general, to say that 'in this particular field [*sc.* education] there is no such thing as proof' (Mary Warnock in Peters, 1973, p. 112). Nevertheless it seems true and useful to say that 'if we are discussing what sort of education is best, we must take into account . . . what educated people think is best, and also, more importantly, whatever it is in education that people ultimately must enjoy, and therefore want' (ibid.); if the first part of this remark seems viciously circular, the last part seems promising. At this point, then, it may be worthwhile to run an argument, at least in outline, which takes its starting-point from the notion of seriousness and not from any predetermined view about the 'value' of particular subjects — whether in terms of a tradition of 'academic standards' or in terms of 'the child's interests'. There are, for fairly obvious reasons, good logical grounds for thinking that seriousness, in itself and other things being equal, is necessarily a valuable or desirable quality; that to be enthusiastic about something, to love it and care for it, to derive pleasure from relating to it and understanding it for what it is, is necessarily a good for man — perhaps a description of *the* good for man. Now a very natural move to make here, if we are concerned about what modes or media ('subjects') we think children might be serious *in*, is the Aristotelian move of looking at what is done by people who are already well-equipped with seriousness, and given a fair chance to cash this quality out in their everyday lives.

This sort of procedure seems to me necessary, if we are to avoid unjustifiable imposition on the one hand or total randomness on the other. For the 'importance' of one subject as against another, in this context — that is, in terms of what pupils can come to love and be serious about, not in terms of what may be socially or otherwise pragmatically useful is ultimately verifiable only in terms of its importance *to a person or people*. The relevant questions are of the form 'Will studying X give this person something he can love? Will it add importantly to his happiness and his consciousness? Will it give him an object of abiding interest and pleasure?', rather than 'Is knowing about X the mark of an "educated man"?' (or of some other kind of man which we favour for conceptual, or moral, or merely cultural reasons). At the same time we have to *answer* the questions *for* the pupil, because people (particularly children) are not always, perhaps not even often, the best judges of what will suit them. Obviously their immediate interests and desires are relevant; even more relevant is whatever knowledge we can acquire about them as people, so that we can make good guesses about what they will 'take to'. In any case, we have to use some criteria for putting certain Xs rather than others in their way; we cannot leave it to chance or fashion.

There is a sort of parallel here with helping pupils to choose jobs. If we leave aside 'external' criteria (whether a particular job pays well, bestows status, etc.) and consider what jobs are likely to give a particular pupil satisfaction simply for what they are in themselves, we should not wish to be governed entirely by some predetermined view about the intrinsic satisfaction of some jobs as against others irrespective of the people doing them. At the same time we should not take immediate interests and desires ('I want to be an engine-driver') as a good guide. We should rather ask questions like 'Is this person the sort of person who will, in fact, find a lot of satisfaction in a *job* at all? (Perhaps he will find most of his happiness in his private life and hobbies.) In so far as he is, what sorts of jobs do people of this psychological type characteristically find most satisfying?' And we should find it helpful, not only to study the psychology of the particular person more closely, but also to look at other people who were not under pressure from 'external' criteria, in order to determine what jobs they chose and stayed with in their lives. We would then have some reason to introduce pupils to those sorts of jobs rather than to others.

I must make it clear that I am not proposing this as the *only* criterion for the practical selection of school subjects. First, as we have already noted, there are many things which all or most children will need to learn for quite down-to-earth reasons, reasons which might be called 'practical', 'utilitarian', or 'social'. Thus, in our society, literacy and a minimum of elementary mathematics seem necessary, and various basic competences might be added — for instance, being able to drive a car or look after a baby. Equally there are obvious reasons why a basic moral education is necessary for pupils in any society; we cannot afford to have too much theft, violence or social disorder. But we can distinguish, if only roughly, between what is learned for reasons of this kind and what is learned for its own sake and in its own right, irrespective of extrinsic or utilitarian reasons. Any man needs some moral or political education as a citizen, but not every man will find it worth while to become a moral philosopher or a political sociologist.

Second, it will of course be impossible for pupils (and, in all probability, for ourselves) to know what subjects they will be seriously attached to unless and until they have some experience of them. This is, again, much like saying that some experience of doing various jobs is, at least, very useful in deciding what job to opt for, or that some experience of the opposite sex is essential in order to determine whom one ought to marry. It is necessary, then, to initiate the pupils to some extent into a number of subjects, in order for him and us to be able to see what really suits him — and, of course, it may suit some pupils to pursue several or many of them, rather than just one: that sort of pursuit may represent the kind of seriousness those pupils have. The point is rather that the criterion for selecting (or defining) the subjects should be what other serious people have found to be worth while.

Naturally it will make a great difference how these subjects are initially presented or taught; what pupils find 'interesting' or 'stimulating' will depend on the teacher. But we are trying to go a bit deeper than this. A life-long commitment to pursuing some subject may be enabled or facilitated by competent or inspiring teaching, but cannot be wholly created by it. The teacher has to mediate, as it were, between the subject itself and whatever (largely unknown and certainly unconscious) forces may or may not drive the pupil to embrace it. This is done, in part, by trying to show the pupil what other people 'see in' the subject, the kind of excitement and weight it has for them, the reasons why it has a long tradition of study (with all the apparatus of professors, university courses, research work and so forth).

For that part of education which consists of pursuing subjects in this way, then, I am arguing that the selection and identification of subjects should be determined in a way which might fairly be described as 'traditional', in that we are to rely on what serious people have traditionally found worth while; rather as, to use another parallel, we rely on the 'test of time' for selecting those works of art, music and literature which we think worthy of our pupils' attention. That is, we select those which perceptive and interested people in the past have in fact found worthy. In other words, we make use of what seems to be the appropriate reference-group.

This suggested move clearly involves us in some consideration of one set of natural candidates for such a reference-group: namely, university teachers and researchers. But we have to be very careful here, for a wide variety of reasons. They are not natural candidates because they are cleverer than other possible groups, such as lawyers or businessmen (doubtful), or because they are more naturally dedicated to learning (more doubtful still), or because they are more earnest and hard-working (very doubtful indeed). It is rather that they represent almost the only group *not under pressure* (or not under much pressure) from utilitarian or 'instrumental' sources. Of course other people are and have been in such favoured situations also. In fact it would be illuminating to consider the case of, say, the eighteenth-century Whig aristocrats, or whatever other cases we could find of people who were able and willing to engage in learning or other activities simply for their own sake.

In particular the use of a university reference-group cannot and should not settle a number of specific questions for us: cannot, because the practice in universities does not all point in the same direction; and should not (even if it did), because it is not our business to settle them − as I shall shortly argue. First, it does not point us towards making our distinctions in terms of 'forms of thought': thus, in so far as the Literae Humaniores course at the University of Oxford is deemed worthy of any respect, this can hardly be because it is restricted to one (logical) type of discipline. Second, it does not point towards 'specialization', if the criterion for 'a subject' is deployed in terms of the ten or so subjects commonly to be found on school timetables. At universities there are *both* people who cover the ground of several such subjects *and* people who cover only a small part of one. Third, it does not point to preferring subjects whose criteria of success are clear and easily demonstrable, as perhaps with mathematics, science and some others: even those at the older universities who have a passion for 'hardness' and clear verifiability, and are (properly) suspicious of the 'soft option' and 'waffle' that may be permitted or engendered by methodologically dubious subjects, would find it hard to state clearly the criteria for, say, 'good literary criticism' or even 'good philosophy'.

As the last point suggests, it is misguided to cash out the kind of merits that universities have in this context — the kind of reliance we can place in them as a reference-group — in such terms as 'specialized', 'hard discipline', 'academic standards', 'centres of excellence', and so on. The point is rather that we have here large numbers of intelligent, serious and non-pressurized people who *find themselves*, as it were, drawn towards certain kinds of questions, or disciplines, or pursuits, or areas of study. These kinds, as we have seen, are extremely heterogeneous; any attempt to delimit them always comes up against resisting cases. The force of using this reference-group is simply to answer the question 'What sorts of things do people of this kind seem naturally to find themselves interested in?' in a quite empirical way.

Of course this is subject to all sorts of qualifications: thus there is the question of what universities to put in our group, or what people in them to take as 'serious', etc.; the fact that many institutions and individuals *are* under pressure, from the outside world or from their own traditions; and many other doubts would occur to us besides. Nevertheless, it is not absurd to rely on this sort of procedure, to identify people whose *life* consists of learning to the best of their ability, whilst leaving it open to them to choose what sort of learning they are going to pursue. The same sort of procedure, incidentally, could be used for selecting activities which are not only or primarily activities of learning. Thus suppose we think it likely that children are to some extent suited by a pursuit falling roughly under the heading of, say, 'indoor games': then, *rather than* attempt to 'justify' some games philosophically as 'more intrinsically valuable', or other games as 'more relevant to the modern world', or whatever, we simply *look and see* what sorts of games are in fact popular with serious grown-up players who have time to play, and are not just playing for money.

It is not, of course, in dispute that we have to allow for such factors as time and ability. Suppose a subject or study-area (S) is such that a lot of people in our reference-group find themselves drawn towards it (see it as 'rewarding'), but also such that it can only *be* 'rewarding' if one is fairly clever and in a position to put in a lot of time working hard at the earlier 'unrewarding' stages (the higher reaches of classical literature might be a candidate for this description). Then, since many pupils are not very clever, and are not likely to have much spare time after they leave school, S will be unsuitable for these pupils. A point such as this is very obvious, and indeed constantly made in educational writing. What I want to stress, however, is that these 'practical' factors have to be considered *in conjunction with* the criterion of selection I am advocating, in a defeasible sort of way: that is, we should say something like 'From our reference-group it appears that S1, S2 and S3 are the sorts of subjects that serious people with time find rewarding, so prima facie we will select these for our children: of course, *if* Johnny is too stupid ever to get properly into S1, or *if* Mary will never have enough time to get into S2, then (alas) we shall have to find something more suitable.'

In fact, the most important limiting factors are likely to be, not so much time or ability, but (as suggested in the last chapter) the amount and quality of the pupils' seriousness itself: 'motivation', if you like. This amount and quality are largely outside our control: they are certainly not, as we sometimes like to think, infinitely negotiable. In practice, therefore, there will be many Ss which are not available to many pupils. To take extreme and perhaps non-controversial cases: nobody seriously supposes that many children will, in the foreseeable future, be able and willing to appreciate Vergil, Proust, or Dante: the differential calculus or the theory of relativity: the philosophy of Kant or the plays of Aeschylus. We must, of course, give the chance to all who can and will, and we must try to increase the number of those who can and will by increasing their seriousness. But the facts have to be faced.

We fail to face these facts if we do not distinguish our Ss with the utmost clarity. We may *call* both the appreciation of Vergil and a school outing to visit Roman baths 'Latin' (wrongly); and we may say that learning to count and learning to do the differential calculus are both part of 'mathematics' (rightly); and also we may invent new subject-titles — 'the environment', 'integrated humanities', and so on (neither rightly nor wrongly, but just confusingly). But *one* important criterion we need to deploy in order to mark different Ss is the criterion of how hard, complex, or advanced they are; how much seriousness they require. Otherwise we shall merely persuade ourselves, falsely, that all our pupils are doing much the same thing.

We mask the truth in a similar way if, on this false presumption, we also fail to make those institutional arrangements which are obviously necessary for different sorts of Ss. The notion, for instance, that a common form of *examination* could conceivably cover Ss that might be marked by, say, 'Latin' or 'English' is clearly delusive: the variety of Ss is too wide. Nor is it a question of pupils studying 'the same thing at different levels'. The difference of level is often, I think almost always, sufficient to make it preferable to say that they are studying different things. Again, it is clear that different sorts of *institutions*, schools, classes or 'sets', teachers, etc., will fit different Ss and the pupils able and willing to learn these Ss as opposed to other Ss. These and similar points, as indeed we noticed in chapter 1, have obvious practical bearings on our educational arrangements.

I hope to have made it clear within what limits this line of argument should operate. To summarize:

1   It ought not to be doubted (though the reasons need lengthier exposition) that people should be serious about some things: that they should enjoy, or find worthwhile, some things for their own sake.

2   Being a serious *learner* – that is, roughly, loving the acquisition and exercise of some mastery or understanding – is one important way in which one can be serious: for education, obviously the most important way.

3   *Among* the things one can seriously learn are those which we can reasonably describe as 'subjects'.

4   *In so far as* we can plausibly view our pupils as serious learners of subjects, an important criterion both for categorizing and for presenting subjects will be the criterion of what serious people, past and present, have found satisfying. This should at least give us some guidance about what *is* satisfying, or suited to natural human interests. To determine this in any *a priori* or theoretical way seems difficult; perhaps impossible, if we are thinking in terms of general laws. It has much to do with the kind of appeal various subjects have for elements of our unconscious minds, which is why we have to allow for some flexibility and choice: for different people's unconscious, as well as conscious, minds are differently structured. But in so far as we have to put *some* things (subjects) rather than others before children, the best we can do is to rely upon a procedure of this kind.

I am suggesting that what we have in the universities (and, of course, elsewhere) is a kind of *tradition of interest* which offers a necessary criterion not just for 'able' or 'academic' pupils but for all pupils, *in so far as* we and they are concerned with serious learning and abiding interest. From this point of view, it is irrelevant that universities may also provide other sorts of traditions – for instance, a tradition of *merit* or 'excellence'. How *competent* particular pupils are, or how likely they are themselves to enter or teach at a university, or what sort of 'progress' or 'standards' they achieve, is only contingently related to what subjects they are *interested* in. (This relationship is very obscure: there is a sort of assumption that pupils are bound to be interested in what they are good at, but even if this is a fair assumption the fact may reflect our particular educational and social system rather than any natural psychological law.)

Even if we had much more serious doubts about universities themselves than those I have already raised, the skeleton of the argument is
not affected. (One could, for instance, identify a group of 'serious students', initiate them into all sorts of subjects and study-areas, put them
on a well-stocked desert island and see what they chose to study: a
fatuous-sounding suggestion, but pointing at least to the need for controlled research to determine what types of study do, in fact, 'suit'
what types of people.) It does, of course, *also* offer us another advan-
tage: that of a tradition of *seriousness* which it is important for pupils
to recognize, whatever their own degree of seriousness may be. For
instance, it seems right that I should say 'Yes, I do enjoy playing chess;
but I'm afraid I'm not really serious about it – if I were, I should learn
all the right openings and so on, like Fischer and Spassky have'; and this
is importantly different from saying 'I enjoy playing chess but I'm not
clever enough to do it properly'. The point here is that it is of great
value that pupils should *get to know*, so far as they can (and we can
help them), how serious they are about various things: and this can be
measured against a tradition as well as in other ways. This is not to
deny that they should also get to know how clever or naturally 'good
at' things they are; but this is a different point, and I think ultimately
a less important one. To use another absurd-sounding example: the best
test for entry to a university might be simply to *leave pupils alone* for a
few months, and see whether they seriously applied themselves to learning of their own free will. If they did, I should be inclined to rate this
higher than any test we now have of their abilities.

As will be apparent, the intent behind this argument is partly to
defuse some common extremist opinions on this topic; and of course it
leaves many important questions untouched. Given that percentage (we
might put it) of the pupil which we are happy to devote to serious
learning, the suggested criterion seems to me of great importance. But
this does not determine the percentage. The important thing, perhaps,
is to distinguish such percentages clearly, along the lines elsewhere suggested (pp. 73ff.). We shall never be able to do this by more than hit-
and-miss procedures until we know far more psychology, and have far
better personal relationships in schools – the latter not only for their
own sakes, but because only by knowing the pupils intimately have we
any real chance of judging the percentages properly.

Apart from this – admittedly rather *ad hoc* – procedure of using
what seems to be the most sensible reference group, all we can do is to
make intelligent guesses about the most important criteria: if only to
suggest some lines for research, or by way of advising teachers what to
look out for. In considering what particular pupils are likely to be
'serious' about (or derive permanent pleasure and enrichment from, or
be permanently attached to, or however we want to describe it) we are,
fairly obviously, talking about the psychology of the unconscious. One

of the chief problems and obstacles to progress here, I think, is how to conceive the questions we want to ask; and words like 'unconscious', associated as they may be in people's minds with other imagery attaching to 'Freud', 'psychoanalysis', 'mental illness', etc. – and perhaps to the whole clinical or medical image which these terms project – may lead us in the wrong direction. It may be better to say that we are interested in *what it is about* various subjects that has force, or magnetism, or significance for various types of people: what they symbolize for them, what *species boni* they unconsciously evoke. Here the idea of subjects being interesting 'in themselves' seems to me a naive one; although of course this idea may be used to contrast, for instance, the person who studies science simply in order to get a better job with the person who is, as we say, 'just interested' in it, or who studies it 'for its own sake'. For clearly there must be *reasons why* he is interested in it, reasons which relate something about science to something about his individual psychology.

Two possible lines of approach seem worth pursuing. First, there may be things about what we might call the content, or (perhaps better) the *material*, of the subject. One may be interested in Greek history because all things Greek have a certain glamour about them: they stand, perhaps, for some romantic world of childhood which one tries to revive. Or, one may find oneself paying a lot of attention to *terrain*, and hence to maps and geography, perhaps for similar reasons: perhaps some post-Freudian analyst will give us a story in which terrain represents the mother's body. We are not talking here of the initial or immediate interest of the subject (indeed 'interest' is rather a bad word), but of why one *loves* it: something very far removed from whether it is immediately 'relevant', 'stimulating' or otherwise acceptable, just as what one feels for an attractive blonde in the street is different from the genuine love of a person. We could, therefore, draw on whatever knowledge of the unconscious is available (mostly, I suspect, from detailed case-histories rather than from overall 'theory') to map out these images or symbols and connect them with aspects of different subjects.

Second, there will be natural preferences for certain *elements* in subjects: for what one might call 'types of work'. Clearly some pupils take to memorizing or rote-learning easily, others to the collection of 'facts', others again to critical analysis, others to giving proofs or reasoning, others to imaginative moves that may be made within the subject, and so on. We are here talking (roughly) about different types of mental operation; and we are badly in need of a serious taxonomy of these. Each type will be preferred by a person for some reason or other: a reason which – if he really likes that sort of work 'in itself' – will necessarily be largely unconscious. Perhaps certain pupils, or pupils at certain ages, badly need to reassure themselves by being in a position where they can get clear 'right answers', or repeat accurately what they have memorized; perhaps others find exactitude restrictive and want scope for their imagination, or conversely take joy in precision but feel bogged down without clear verification-procedures.

All this, I am well aware, is extremely vague; but the job badly needs to be done. It will not, of course, follow even from this that we shall want to use no *other* criterion. There will be times when we shall wish to supplement, or compensate for, a child's 'natural' attachments to certain material or certain elements; perhaps for general psychological reasons (for instance, to prevent him from becoming obsessive), or perhaps because we can produce other kinds of arguments for the value of certain subjects — arguments which do not rely on this sort of attachment. But at least we shall know when we are likely to be working with or against the grain, so to speak; at least our insight will be better informed. Good teachers, like good parents, deploy this kind of insight already, in so far as they are able and willing to know their pupils intimately. All that the theorist can do is to suggest to them one or two ways of considering the problem of subject-selection which they might not already have thought of — and it is clear that these will also apply to the *presentation* of different subjects ('teaching-methods', if you like). For most subjects can be viewed in the light of most of the criteria we have mentioned, and presented accordingly. Perhaps the most important thing here is for the teacher to keep the game open: not to fall victim to facile dichotomies between 'traditional' and 'progressive' methods, or attach doctrinaire plus or minus values to 'rote-learning', 'divergent thinking', and so on. It may be that in time educational theory will have something more solid to offer than passing phases of fashion.

Chapter seven

Autonomy

In recent years teachers and student-teachers have been deluged with a large number of apparently new ideas, marked with such terms of art as 'creativity', 'critical thinking' and 'autonomy': at least these three, and the greatest of these seems to be 'autonomy'. The term is invariably used with approval, if also nebulously. It is slightly more surprising that nearly all contemporary philosophers of education echo or at least acquiesce in the approval (for example, Hirst and Peters, 1970, p. 40), though the nebulosity remains. I shall argue here that there is, perhaps, *one* concept plausibly marked by the term which is educationally important, but that this comes nowhere near the terrain round which the word usually hovers. Wider questions, about what our general attitude to such terms of art should be, may be more profitably deferred until we have had a look at another such term, 'creativity', in the next chapter.

I shall use one tolerably clear and sensible article on the topic as a starting-point. Dearden (Dearden *et al.*, 1972, p. 453) says that a person is autonomous

> to the degree that what he thinks and does in important areas of his life cannot be explained without reference to his own activity of mind. . . . That is to say, the explanation of why he thinks and acts as he does in these areas must include a reference to his own choices, deliberations, decisions, reflections, judgments, plannings or reasonings. . . . By contrast, there are at least two possible sorts of heteronomy. Firstly, a man's thoughts and actions may be governed by other people. . . . A second form of heteronomy would consist in a man's being governed by factors which are, in a sense, in himself, but which are nevertheless external to his activity of mind. Examples of this sort of heteronomy might include the various forms of psychosis and perhaps also neurosis.

One's first reaction to this, I think, would be to wonder how what a man 'thinks and does' *could ever* 'be explained without reference to his own activity of mind'. Indeed it is tempting, if not always linguistically proper, to enforce a necessary link between anything properly to be called 'doing' (as against things that happen to a man) and some notion of intention, or belief, or rule-following; and 'thinking' might be an even better candidate. If this is what 'autonomy' is to mean, are not people always autonomous?

Clearly 'his own activity of mind' must bear a narrower sense, a sense in which it is possible for 'a man's thoughts and actions' to be 'governed by other people' (or by 'psychosis' and perhaps 'neurosis', both of which are demonstrably part of one's 'activity of mind', this is why the phrase is so useless). Now we should normally count under the rubric of 'governed by other people' a very large number of different cases. For example:

1 the case where I am in a Nazi concentration camp (and devote a great deal of 'reflections, judgments, plannings' and so on to survival);
2 the case where I obey the established political authorities and laws, whether or not I have given any consent to these;
3 the case where I take the advice of some authority or expert – a doctor or an architect;
4 the case where, as a loving father, what I do is largely determined by the wants of my wife and family.

Even more heterogeneous would be the cases which arose from bringing in the (cloudy) notions of 'psychosis' and 'neurosis'. Are all, some, or none of these cases to count as 'heteronomy'?

In trying to answer this, we need to remember that 'autonomy' is supposed by Dearden and others to be a *good* thing; and nobody, I imagine, wants to say that (for instance) taking expert advice and acting on it, or becoming an apprentice rather than pretending to be already a craftsman, represents undesirable behaviour, to be downgraded under the heading of 'heteronomy'. But this point cuts deeper than is often supposed. Suppose we describe – too vaguely, but it will do for now – a move as 'putting oneself in someone else's hands', or a state of affairs as 'being in someone else's hands', and think of all the cases of this that are possible. Then it is clear that the desirability of this is something we can hardly generalize about at all: almost everything will depend on the particular position. I may be a spastic or an ancient Spartan; even if there are no operative reasons of a social or technical kind for making this move, it may still suit me psychologically – to a greater or lesser extent, and in different areas of life. It is hardly clear what would be *meant* by saying that *in general* people ought (or ought not) to make this move, or be educated to make it.

It seems clear, nevertheless, that Dearden (together with most contemporary educators) does, in fact, think that there is a generalization to be made here. If so, the first thing to be said is that this must presumably be an empirical generalization — and surely something about which we should expect psychologists and sociologists, rather than philosophers, to inform us. Actually Dearden tries both a conceptual and an empirical line. The first emerges in (ibid., p. 460):

> The accomplishment of what we want or intend, under the description embodied in the intention, is necessarily a satisfaction, and our satisfaction is the greater the more there is of what we intend in what we accomplish.

Whether or not this is true (surely wants and intentions often turn out badly, when we pursue 'apparent goods', as Aristotle would say, and are hence dissatisfied rather than satisfied), it does no substantive job. For people very often want and intend to put themselves, or be, in someone else's hands: to be told what to do, to have their lives organized for them, perhaps even just to stop having to think and plan and decide. Nevertheless Dearden at once continues (ibid.):

> Empirical substantiation of this is abundantly available in human action from the earliest years. Even the youngest children enjoy 'doing it for themselves' and resent being 'bossed'. . . .

But this leap back into the empirical only reminds one of counter-cases: young children, and perhaps they *par excellence*, seem often to want and certainly often need a firm disciplinary structure, government by other people, etc. And perhaps Aristotle was right in thinking that the same is true of women and others with 'servile mentalities', however much current fashion is against it.

In any case, the points that emerge, if 'autonomy' and 'heteronomy' are in any way to be construed along the broad lines above ('being in someone else's hands'), are (1) 'autonomy' will not always be a good thing, nor 'heteronomy' a bad one; (2) what particular régimes, situations, etc. actually suit what sorts of people is an empirical question, to which there is clearly no simple answer (cf. chapter 4, pp. 56ff.). So we are driven to seek some other interpretation. The most obvious, which certainly runs through Dearden's thinking as well as Kant's, is the idea of being governed by 'reason' or 'rationality' rather than by anything else. But *prima facie*, on this interpretation, the autonomous man who realizes that his life would be most happy and fruitful if spent under close supervision would join the army (or whatever) and remain in it without losing his autonomy, even though almost the whole of his life might consist of obeying other people's orders. This is certainly a very different picture from the one painted earlier, in terms (roughly) of the sort of régime or structure of a man's life: the earlier picture would probably count a butler or Spartan hoplite as 'heteronomous', and perhaps a successful writer or artist as 'autonomous' — whereas if we tie autonomy to rationality none of this necessarily follows.

One does not need to explore here what might be meant by saying that a man's life should be governed by 'reason' or 'what is rational' in order to see a clear, indeed over-obvious, link with education. It is hardly in dispute that education, at least to some degree, should be concerned with getting children to understand and act on 'good reasons' as these apply in various spheres and departments of knowledge and life. Dearden does not, however, pursue possible conceptual connections between autonomy and reason, except in a (very proper) attempt to show that, *pace* certain existentialists, 'Reason is not . . . a threat to autonomy' (ibid., p. 459). Indeed, he specifically *separates* autonomy ('not the only thing that matters') from both 'morality' and 'respect for truth' (ibid., p. 460). So the idea is not, apparently, that we are only to speak of 'autonomy' when what a man does is in accordance with moral goodness or truth: 'Great criminals are markedly autonomous men' (ibid., p. 461). For Dearden, reason seems to connect with autonomy only by virtue of the idea that the autonomous man will do a lot of reasoning ('deliberations, decisions', etc.). In his earlier writing (Dearden, 1968, pp. 46ff.) the line seems to be different. The 'central values' of 'an ideal of personal autonomy based on reason' are said to be 'independence, reason, integrity, truth, freedom of individual choice and judgment concerning what is worthwhile, responsibility, and fairness' (ibid., p. 47). (I should add here that I have also had the benefit of reading more recent papers by Dearden and Elizabeth Telfer under the heading 'Autonomy as an Educational Ideal': I have not referred to these in detail, since my main points are not affected.)

Other authors also display some uncertainty about this connection. Thus Peters writes that the autonomous person 'is not prepared to accept authoritative pronouncements' (Peters, 1966, p. 196); and as this remark stands (that is, if he really means 'authoritative' rather than, say, 'dictatorial') it suggests that the autonomous person can be bloody-minded or stiff-necked or just stupid. Again, 'Autonomy implies the ability and determination to regulate one's life by rules which one has accepted for oneself — presumably because the reasons for them are both apparent and convincing' (ibid., p. 197); but now, either the notion of 'accepting for oneself' is going to extend further than we want it to (so that bloody-mindedness is not excluded), or else we have to add some such clause as 'when it's reasonable to do so'.

This latter is certainly the most natural line to take with 'autonomy'. The word is to name a virtue, a certain disposition to act in accordance with right reason: it would be the opposite of notions perhaps marked by 'servility', and located somewhere in the area of 'thinking for one-self', 'independent-minded', 'having a capacity for self-direction', etc. Such a line, however, has difficulties of its own, arising from an *embarras de richesse*. There is, first, a problem which crops up with many virtue-words: that is, does 'autonomy' refer primarily to certain types of what we may roughly call 'behaviour-patterns', or to the ability to resist certain standard temptations (or to some mixture of these)? In either alternative, it seems that the cases which we – or at least the current literature – would want to put under 'autonomy' are too heterogeneous to accommodate a single concept. (Peters, 1974, pp. 340–2, says a little about these differences under the headings of 'authenticity', 'rational reflection' and 'strength of will'. I don't dis-agree with what he says, but the general impression of uncertainty about what to do with 'autonomy' reinforces the point I am trying to make here.) Thus, in the first alternative, it seems to be one thing to throw off a tyrant's yoke in a political situation, another thing to work out one's own moral problems, another thing again not to become anxious if one's work or personal relationships are not tightly struc-tured, and yet another thing to have good rather than bad reasons for demonstrating against a South African rugby tour (I have taken all these examples from the literature). In the second alternative, it seems that these and other examples of behaviour might occur because a per-son was too fearful, *or* too lazy, *or* too easily impressed, *or* too anxious to succeed with his endeavour, or as a result of plenty of other tempta-tions.

One would not, then, be easily convinced that there is a sufficient homogeneity in such cases to justify the erection of 'autonomy' as a new virtue. Of course one may talk vaguely of 'family resemblances', and people may erect what concepts they will and mark them by what-ever words they choose; but there is certainly no *clear* enough account to satisfy us, and to justify the constant use of the word (as if we all knew what it meant). What may have happened, I think, is that there has been too hasty a borrowing from where the word has a natural and non-metaphorical home, in its earliest and most common use – that is, referring to states or communities who are sovereign and have the power of making their own laws. Subsequent uses, including Kant's (and Piaget's), are metaphorical or at best analogous; and one of the difficulties of the metaphor is precisely that no question of *psychologi-cal* characteristics enters into the autonomy of states and communities – and also that no questions are begged concerning the *desirability* of their autonomy. At least we can say, without too much difficulty, how far Texas or Andorra or the USA are autonomous states: nothing fol-lows from this, either about whether they eagerly seize the chance of making lots of laws of their own (as against remaining inert and timid), or about whether it might not in fact be better for them to resign their sovereignty and put themselves in someone else's hands. We could, of course, take the same line with personal autonomy: to assess a man's autonomy would then be simply to assess to what extent he could — and 'could' here will refer exclusively or at least primarily just to legal rights and entitlements — run his own life, free from the rules or pressures of government or other social groups. But then we should be talking about political freedom in some sense or other, not about an aim of education.

Even if it were possible (as perhaps it may be) to delimit a virtue, to be called 'autonomy', along the lines described above — that is, roughly, 'thinking and doing things for oneself when it is reasonable to do so' — it seems to me plain (though the vagueness of the literature leaves me a little uncertain) that this is not the line that defenders or proponents of autonomy in fact want to take. If we took this line, one might also want to propound another virtue — this time less original — to take care of all the cases where people 'do things for themselves' where it is *not* reasonable — when they are bloody-minded or stiff-necked or just stupid. We might talk here of 'obedience', or borrow Plato's notion of 'each man doing his proper work'. In drawing attention to these (still extremely misty) virtues, we should be demonstrating, as it were, the operation of reason or the rational man in certain specific contexts or spheres, or in facing certain temptations — perhaps, if we worked it out properly, in both conjointly. This, I am sure, would be well worth doing; but it is not what merchants of autonomy want to do. They want to propose it as a much more substantive ideal; something which therefore needs defence, rather than as an aspect of rational behaviour.

The literature gives various indications of this. There is, for instance, Dearden's idea that a person should at least be autonomous 'in the more important areas of his life': this to include 'work and domestic life', not 'decisions about catching buses' (Dearden *et al.*, 1972, p. 453). Again, Hirst and Peters raise the question 'But on what grounds is autonomy singled out as a desirable state?' (Hirst and Peters, 1970, p. 40), and later 'What arguments can the lover of liberty advance against the kindly despot who puts more emphasis on the virtues of conformity and obedience?' (ibid., p. 41). These are, they say, 'moral questions that require an answer' in further philosophical work: as authors who have put forward a particular notion of education, 'They are conscious that a definite moral point of view is implicit in their approach' (ibid.). In other words, they just believe (for whatever reasons) that 'autonomy' is a good thing: and this belief, if I interpret them fairly, seems somehow to involve the idea that the more that a man thinks or does for himself, the better. The questions are, first, whether any sense can be made of this: and second, why it should be thought desirable.

One notion which, in a way, answers both questions at once, derives from a certain picture of education, very familiar from the writings of current philosophers in the field. To take a simple case: the pupil who understands why the answer to a mathematical question is such-and-such, because he has worked it out for himself, shows signs of being (*pro tanto*) more educated than the pupil who just obeys orders to write down the answer, or looks it up in the back of the textbook, or copies it from his neighbour. Similarly, the man who understands the point of moral principles and makes his own decisions on that basis is more 'morally educated' than the man who just accepts tradition or peer-group pressure. On this notion of education, at least, descriptions of 'being educated' will be descriptions of activities which a man must, logically, 'do for himself': activities of which it will *make no sense* to say that 'someone else can do it for him'. (The clearest case is perhaps the appreciation of the arts.)

The *sense* of 'autonomy', if we take this line, will then be cashed out in terms of these descriptions; and the *value* of autonomy will depend on how far the described activities are thought desirable. Because of the close link with 'being educated', it will be possible to swap various terms around at will. For instance, Dearden allows autonomy to the political demonstrator if he has 'sincerely held views', makes relevant distinctions, is immune to 'the rhetoric of some opinion leader, the mood of a crowd or an unconscious wish to fight authority', and so on (Dearden *et al.*, 1972, p. 455), and this is just another way of saying that he demonstrates 'with understanding', 'reasonably', 'as a result of being educated', 'in a sensible and well-informed spirit', or whatever.

On this interpretation, then, a man will think and act 'autonomously' to the extent and degree that his thought and actions are conducted with understanding, 'awareness', or (to use a jargon term in the literature) 'cognitive perspective'. He must, so to speak, not just push buttons but know something of how the machine works. Possibly this interpretation may fit Dearden's paraphrase: 'to the degree that what he thinks and does cannot be explained without reference to his own activity of mind'. But, as we have seen, this paraphrase is certainly too wide; judging autonomy will be more a matter of assessing the 'activity of mind' itself (as indeed Dearden sees in the political demonstration case and elsewhere). In the same way, 'doing things with understanding' will not always overlap with what will, in many cases, be the most natural interpretation of 'doing things for oneself' or even 'thinking for oneself'. In some cases (like the 'education' ones), where the 'doing' or task precisely *is* to deploy understanding, of course there will be a (logically necessary) overlap; and in some other cases, one might want to argue that 'doing things for oneself' is a contingently necessary condition for the development of understanding (as, for instance, it might be held that a Samuel-Smiles or Robinson-Crusoe régime for bringing up children in fact led to more understanding than a régime based on classrooms and textbooks). But in other cases a do-it-yourself programme will not necessarily either develop or overlap with such understanding.

I do not think this interpretation worth pursuing: partly because it is too logically snug to give us the substantive (and therefore questionable) ideal we seem to require, and partly because it throws the substantive question back to the value of 'understanding', 'cognitive perspective', 'education' (in the sense mentioned above) and so on in general. Assessment of the whole 'package deal' is certainly important; but it represents only *one* option, or one specification for the content of education. A broader concept, such as that deployed in chapter 1, would not so tailor the content that 'autonomy' is a necessary part of the package: one can learn, in a 'serious and sustained' fashion, *both* to 'think for oneself' *and* to obey orders.

My guess is that the basic ideas floating through the (conscious and unconscious) minds of those who advocate autonomy are closely bound up with a particular notion of moral freedom (perhaps one should include political freedom), which is then extended into other areas of life. This notion is argued for by many philosophers (notoriously by Kant) and may still be the prevailing orthodoxy today: it stands, for instance, in obvious contrast to some of the ideas in Plato's *Republic*. Central to this notion is the belief that there can be no 'moral experts' (whatever this may mean); and that there is a sharp distinction between choosing one's ends, 'values' or principles on the one hand, which one can only do for oneself', and hiring experts or taking advice about means to those ends on the other hand. All this, of course, is as yet very sketchy and unclear; but we can already see how certain areas might be demarcated both as what Dearden might allow as 'important' — one's ends, basic 'values', chief goals and interests in life, and as areas in which, since there are no experts, it would be not only servile and undignified but also unreasonable not to be 'autonomous'.

I do not myself find any of the arguments advanced in favour of this notion either clear or convincing; but in such a vast topic the best I can do is to try to clarify a few muddles, and see in what state such clarification leaves the notion of autonomy. The following points seem relevant in particular:

1 We have first to distinguish sharply between (a) the notion of basic or initial *consent to* a régime or style of life, and (b) the *nature of* the régime. Men may freely consent to a dictatorship and a totalitarian or hierarchical society, or be forced or in various ways pressurized into a type of society describable as 'liberal' or 'democratic'. There may, perhaps, be reasons of strict logic why the notion of free negotiation and initial consent should be upheld as more important (because logically prior) than the content of any régime, life-style, political set-up or

philosophical theory (chapter 4, pp. 58ff.). But is this all that proponents of autonomy want? Suppose that, after due discussion and other procedures, the members of some society freely opt to run a system essentially like that advocated by Plato. As an advocate of freedom, I should myself say that they had the right to do this (they should not be forcibly prevented from doing so, if that is their free option); that it would be, nevertheless, an ill-advised exercise of their option; and that, if this happened, advocates of autonomy would not feel that their substantial ideal had been realized. They might well feel in a quandary about such a situation; but for them, I think, 'autonomy' extends beyond the notion of consent. They would object on the grounds that the guardians in Plato's state were perhaps autonomous, but that the rest of the citizens were not.

2 This objection is not supposed to rely only on pragmatic considerations — for instance, Dearden's dislike of being 'bossed' which the citizens might feel, or the difficulties of ensuring in practice that the rulers were both wise and benevolent, or the dangers of the 'blue-print' type of social engineering to which Popper (1966) and others so passionately object. If we confine ourselves to the pragmatic, we shall in fairness have to note all the social contexts in which some such structure is obviously demanded by the need for survival — say, on a warship or in ancient Sparta: and then, as we have sufficiently seen earlier, no generalizations will be possible. The objection is supposed to rest upon some logical thesis, e.g. that 'Ethical and political disagreement is radical and interminable in a sense in which scientific disagreement, or disagreement about the means for achieving an agreed end, is terminable by recognized procedures' or that 'the answers to ethical and political questions do not embody knowledge, and are not such that to each of the questions there is one incontrovertibly true or correct answer' (Bambrough, 1956, p. 109): or perhaps some thesis about 'the language of morals' of a Humean or Harean kind.

There is a short way to be taken with all such theses, the simplicity of which has perhaps caused it to be neglected. Either the 'answers' to moral and political questions are arbitrary, in the sense that one answer is as good as another (in which case we might not want to speak of 'answers' to 'questions' at all); or there will be a sense in which some answers are right (or better, or wiser, or saner, or more reasonable, or by some criteria more satisfactory than others). To put this in another, perhaps more relevant, way: either one man's opinion is as good as another's, or else there are criteria by which we can fairly judge some people to be 'better placed' (to use the most general term I can think of) than others to pronounce on such questions. What being 'better placed' consists in is open to question, and might involve great heterogeneity (for example, the possession of certain concepts, or having faced such issues before, or being cleverer, or more benevolent, or more 'empathetic', or just being on the spot at the time) — nothing is being said now to tie this down more tightly (cf. Barrow, 1974, 1975).

The latter way of formulating the dichotomy may be preferable, because it enables us to by-pass at least some of the arguments about the criteria for settling moral issues (or issues about 'ends'). There is a parallel here with aesthetics: it is plainly possible to hold that some people (literary critics, etc.) are better judges of works of art than other people are, without having to be totally clear about 'how to prove' that a work of art has such-and-such qualities. In the same way we may (particularly after reading too much contemporary moral philosophy) feel thoroughly confused about the precise application of reason to moral issues; yet it would require (I hope) more than the arguments of philosophers to persuade us that notions like wisdom, judgment, understanding, insight, etc. in the field of morality were totally empty.

Either, then, matters are arbitrary (in which case 'autonomy' will mean just 'random selection', which nobody wants to defend): or else it is in principle possible to identify 'moral experts' — perhaps panels of experts, if we believed (as is surely right) that solutions of moral problems required a number of very *different* skills, dispositions, aptitudes, capacities and expertises (for a list with annotations, see Wilson, 1973). And if so, 'autonomy' in respect of morals and politics will be in essentially the same position as 'autonomy' in other areas or forms of thought. That is, in so far as we want right answers to the question 'What shall I do?', and in so far as we can get such answers with more ease and less chance of error from others than from our own labours, what merit is there in being 'autonomous'?

3 All this may sound too simple to be believed; and at once we shall feel a temptation to give descriptions of 'morality' ('ends', 'values', 'ultimate commitments', etc.) such that considerations of *getting right answers* are down-graded. From this point of view, philosophical defendants of 'autonomy' in morals have chosen to bat on a bad wicket by taking 'morality' as centrally or solely concerned with *action*. It is abdundantly clear, *pace* any total relativists that still happen to be around, that many things which people *do* — and we do not have to quote Hitlerian extremes — are unreasonable, misguided, mistaken and incorrect; they tell too many lies, kill other people pointlessly, steal from them unnecessarily, torture them counter-productively, and so forth. For the most part, it is correct to say that any even moderately benevolent, sensible, intelligent and well-informed panel of men could simply *tell* them that these things were wrong, and suggest better alternatives. What such a panel would find it much harder to do would include such enterprises as getting them to *see why* it was unreasonable, arranging their dispositions so that they came to have certain *feelings*

directed towards certain targets and got rid of other feelings, and so on.

But 'getting the right thing done' (as we may safely describe it, by omitting any notions of intention, reason and feeling that may lie behind the complex business of human action) is obviously very important. We are, of course, concerned with *educating* people in morality; but we are also concerned that people should not be killed or beaten up, stolen from, and so forth. Here morality is absolutely on a par with other areas: it is important that people should be educated in science, but also important that bridges should not collapse and that medicines should work. And if 'morality' is made by definition to stand for some area of greater moment than others, the same applies: if it is even more desirable that men should be educated in morality than in other subjects, it will also be even more desirable that we should 'get the right thing done' in morality — indeed, there will surely be a connection between the two.

Further, any interpretation of 'autonomy' which neglected this would also suffer by neglecting another type of submission to moral expertise. For the 'experts', if and when they can be satisfactorily identified, will not only tell one what to do: they will also function as *teachers*, and the person who wants (and is able) to understand things for himself will, if sensible, submit himself to such instruction; again, as with any other subject. This consideration will apply, incidentally, even to areas where *action* is not much involved. A teacher (if the word is appropriate) of musical appreciation or 'personal relationships' may not want or need to tell one what to *do*, but has nevertheless to be respected as somebody who is well-qualified to change one's feelings and perceptions in the right direction.

I do not, of course, claim that there is no more to be said on these and other points: but I do claim that they are enough to upset the idea that there is something untouchable or *toto caelo* different about moral and political thought and action, such that any special notion of autonomy can be founded on the difference. Far too much has been made of a supposed distinction between the *technai* — specialities one can be 'good at' — and 'morality', which is supposed to be concerned with 'the whole man' and 'the good man'. Of course there are distinctions to be made: but 'the whole man' — that is, many of his dispositions and many elements of his character — enters into plenty of other fields besides morality, and conversely there are very many specialized skills and abilities which are relevant to moral thought and action. When we get down to sorting this out (which will involve determining what ground 'morality' is to cover), we shall need a much more sophisticated set of distinctions than the ones we are accustomed to use.

To speak more practically, it seems to me that there is nothing at all absurd or objectionable in the idea that a great many people in the world would be well-advised to act on advice (rather than 'doing it themselves' or even 'thinking for themselves'), even — perhaps particularly in Dearden's 'important' areas of their lives. For instance, what sort of job they would be best suited for, what sort of government they should have, even (if we could find good enough psychotherapists with enough time) what sort of personal and sexual relationships they would be happiest with. Only a Luciferian notion of 'dignity' would lead one to think, with Dearden (Dearden *et al.*, 1972, p. 461), that (say) a 'heteronomous' Spartan soldier, a well-placed footman, or a cobbler who stuck to his last lacked dignity, just because they did not happen to be the best judges of what suited them by way of a station in life; one might equally say that a philosopher wrestling with his sparking-plugs lacked dignity because he had eventually to consult a mechanic who knew more about it than he did.

One may still feel tempted to say something like 'Yes, but it would be nice if these people did also think for themselves and develop their own understanding — surely "autonomy" can still stand for an ideal.' But nobody wants to dispute that *some* value can be attached to 'understanding' ('being educated', etc.); only, we must *also* attach some value to being obedient or sensible enough to 'get the right thing done' — both for oneself and for other people. Certainly nothing has been said to justify the listing of 'autonomy' in the literature of 'educational aims', if it is to stand by itself (or alongside other, perhaps connected, notions from the same stable, such as 'critical thinking', 'creativity', and so on) and without 'obedience' as a co-partner.

I suspect also that a strong reinforcement for much that is said about 'autonomy', as construed above, comes from an uncritical acceptance of some notion of Piagetian 'stages of development'. Without going too deeply into this very complex area (I have made a few points elsewhere in Wilson, 1973, pp. 13ff), we can easily see how this may have happened. Suppose one thought that (a) the notion of children moving up some fixed ladder of 'developmental stages' in 'morality' was conceptually clear, and (b) that there was clear evidence that this actually happened.* Then one might find oneself saying something like 'What "stage" do we want our children to end up in? The earlier, less rational, "heteronomous" stage, or the final stage of "autonomy" or "rational altruism"? Surely the "autonomous" stage, which is "developmentally"

---

*Both these suppositions, particularly (a), seem to me badly mistaken. Nevertheless, plenty of people seem to make them — including reputable philosophers (see for example, Hirst and Peters, 1970, pp. 46ff.). I think the reinforcement for 'autonomy' is detectable in such passages as (Peters, 1966, p. 197).

Autonomy implies the ability and determination to regulate one's life by rules which one has accepted for oneself — presumably because the reasons for them are both apparent and convincing. Piaget has shown that such an attitude towards rules is generally impossible before the age of about seven.

This seems to me wholly incredible.

superior.' Among the many dangers in this picture is the idea that we have somehow to plump for *one* psychological 'type' – either we produce 'heteronomous' people, who may make good soldiers or unquestioning fillers of other publicly-defined roles, or else we produce 'autonomous' people who always think things out for themselves: and then we may find ourselves having to defend 'autonomy' as some specific and questionable moral idea opposed to 'conformity' or 'obedience'.

But to rely on the terminology of the developmental psychologists leads merely to chaos. We just have to go back and say 'If by "autonomy" you mean simply "being reasonable in the moral sphere", then of course we want this sort of person; but then it is often reasonable to put oneself in someone else's hands, and this is not a specific and questionable moral ideal. If by "heteronomy" you mean something which implies "using and acting on the wrong sorts of reasons in morality", then of course heteronomy is (*pro tanto*) a bad thing. On the other hand, if you use "autonomy" even in cases where it is silly to do things for oneself, and "heteronomy" even in cases where it is sensible to obey orders unquestioningly (or whatever), then "autonomy" is not a word for a virtue at all, nor "heteronomy" a word for a vice.'

It is perhaps historically unfortunate that the Kantian and Piagetian tradition has resulted in connecting the term 'autonomy' specifically with morality. For in so far as sense can be made of the notion of 'developmental stages' at all (and this would be chiefly a matter of eliciting conceptual points about the structure of different kinds of knowledge or reasoning) (see Hirst and Peters, 1970, pp. 46ff. and Wilson, 1972a, pp. 15ff), precisely the same moves can be made with regard to other 'forms of thought': indeed one can be more or less 'autonomous' or 'heteronomous' as a chess-player, depending (presumably) on how far one worked things out for oneself as against taking advice from books or bystanders. Here again, of course, there is *a* value in 'autonomy'; and one which, for educationalists (on most definitions of 'education'), is conceptually necessary, being neither more nor less than the value of learning, or understanding, or some aspects of rationality. On this interpretation, it would make no sense to say that we wanted pupils to become good at playing chess (science, mathematics, etc.) but that we did not care whether they were 'autonomous'. But such an interpretation is hardly of interest.

If there is an educational point to be made with 'autonomy', it will be something to do with educating children to realize the force of Kant's injunction to treat people always as ends and not as means. This would be part of moral education, not an aim of education in general. It is, actually, not at all easy to state and defend a clear position even here, and philosophers constantly overreach themselves in trying to do so: thus Hirst and Peters castigate the notion that 'People are thought to be *generally* superior or inferior as human beings' (Hirst and Peters, 1970, p. 91). Here again, either things are wholly arbitrary and nothing would *count as* 'a good man' or 'a better man than I am', or else we do indeed think that some criteria could operate; for instance, it seems to me that if a person were dwarfish, stupid, weak, malevolent, cowardly, unjust, etc. (and one can add anything one likes here), it would be extremely odd to say that he was *not* 'generally inferior' as a human being. By 'odd' I don't mean, or at least don't *have* to mean, logically self-contradictory or strictly nonsensical; maybe the logic of 'a good man' is such that one could say this without formal contradiction. But nor do I mean that it would be just unusual to say this. I mean rather that one could not say it with any show of reason. Not just anything counts as a good reason for commendation, if only because the concept of what you commend is not infinitely plastic. Only certain things could reasonably count as merits or demerits in a man, because only certain things count as being a man: to commend *a man* for being speechless, brutish or irrational makes no sense. Of course this needs (and has had) much more discussion; but generally speaking I think Plato and his followers were right about this, Hume and his followers wrong.

Later Hirst and Peters talk more plausibly of 'human beings deserving to be treated with dignity as becomes any human being'; and presumably points we might want to get across to children under 'autonomy' would lie somewhere in the area of similarities in all rational creatures which are, for certain purposes, crucial. Just what these points are is an immensely difficult question. I think myself that they have to do with a certain kind of equality ('autonomy' if you like) which arises from the fact that human wants, options, and intentions are logically prior to (and generate) any particular use of criteria, reasons, theories or social arrangements. Others may find the relevant points under headings like 'universalisability', 'justice', and so on.

It is certainly not within the scope of this essay to go further into such matters, and I will conclude with what is really a point of methodology. What I hope to have shown is that 'autonomy' has been used as a newly-painted peg on which to hang various hopes and feelings that, when analysed, turn out to be both confused and uninstructive. Briefly, there is nothing here that we do not already know, and a good deal that may induce us to forget what we do already know. My suspicion is that the same is likely to be true for many terms of art similarly brandished (cf. 'child-centred', 'open-ended', 'critical thinking', and so on). The likelihood lies in the very high probability that *ordinary English* (or any other natural language of a tolerably sophisticated kind) will already contain whatever concepts and distinctions we need, if only we have the patience to attend to them (cf. Harré and Secord, 1972): for we are not, after all, dealing with a highly-specialized science that needs its technical terms. Only the baleful influence of a naively behaviouristic psychology would make anyone suppose otherwise. We *know*, so long as we keep our heads, that we want children both to learn to think for themselves, and to learn to be obedient and properly submissive; and we also — again, so long as we keep our heads — have a fairly clear idea, even without the benefit of philosophy, of what we mean by this, and how we would handle most cases that arose in this area. Philosophy here cannot do much more than demolish the products of fantasy: however, this may be the most important task in the fairyland of 'educational theory'.

Chapter eight

Creativity

Most contemporary philosophers of education have been far more severe about 'creativity' than about 'autonomy'; and I should like to couple this chapter with the last, for the sake of an important methodological contrast which we may examine later. It will be best to begin by looking at the way in which (as I believe) some philosophers seem to have missed whatever useful points or concepts may lie behind the word – a way which, incidentally, turns out to have some significance for one's concept of education in general.

Dearden, for instance, says that 'at least four senses of the word are commonly found being run together. First, creativity may simply mean [*sic*] crude self-expression: . . . A second sense of creativity . . . equates it with not falling below a certain minimal rationality in what one says and does. . . . In yet a third sense, creative means "original" ' (1968, pp. 147ff.). It is not made clear what the fourth sense is supposed to be, though later remarks might lead one to guess at some such meaning as 'aesthetically meritorious' (ibid., p. 149, para. 2. I am uncertain whether or not this paragraph redeems the author's promise to give us a fourth 'sense').

It is very difficult to take this as it stands. Whatever we are to do with the term, nobody can really believe that his first two 'senses' – 'crude self-expression' and 'not falling below a certain minimal rationality' – are plausible candidates for a translation or paraphrase. 'Original' is a bit better, though not good enough – any teacher who used the word at all would certainly say that a pupil was being 'creative' when he was not necessarily producing anything which was, by public standards, 'original'. (I would like not to think that 'aesthetically meritorious' is in fact Dearden's fourth 'sense', since his own opening remark under this heading is 'Perhaps the first point worth making about creativity is that it is not confined to the arts' (ibid., p. 146).)

What this author is really worried about emerges more clearly in another writer's longer treatment (White, in Dearden *et al.*, 1972,

111

pp. 132ff.). Both are laudably anxious that teachers should keep a firm grip on *public standards of merit*, as against allowing or encouraging their pupils to do just *anything*. So 'creative' is to mean something like 'meritorious': White says ' "Creative" is a medal which we pin on public products, not the name of private processes' (ibid., p. 136). The trouble, again, is that the word is not in fact used like that at all. We do not say 'That's a very creative symphony', 'What a creative book *War and Peace* is!', and so on. What we most naturally talk about is a *person's* 'creative powers': hence (admittedly more artificially or inflatedly) about 'creative' people or a person's 'creativity'. If we had to say what *sort* of thing 'creativity' was, the most natural reply would be something like 'a power of the mind': and a 'creative' person would be one who had or used this power more than other people. Presumably references to this in education would be references to the acquisition of such powers by learning.

White will have none of this. He criticizes 'an answer frequently found in educational writings', which talks of 'the "creative process" ', 'some innately given power related in some intimate but obscure way to our unconscious mind' ('mind', a slip for 'minds': I don't think White is committing educational writers to some Jungian belief in the collective unconscious). 'It is a power which thrives on exercise but withers away if checked', and so on. Making some allowance for parody, I cannot see that this 'answer' is, as White calls it, 'a fairy story'. His objection is that this is a piece of 'faculty psychology', 'today largely outmoded', which 'rests on a pictorial model of a mind as some sort of ghostly machine with different parts', etc., and claims Ryle as having exploded all this (ibid., pp. 132–4). Later we have something that looks a bit more like an argument: 'If "creative" were a psychological term, describing inner faculties and processes, we could not properly apply the term to Shakespeare, Newton, etc. without knowing what sorts of things went on in their minds as they worked out their masterpieces . . . "creative thinking", therefore, is not a peculiar type of thinking that has different, non-publicly observable features from other types of thinking' (ibid., p. 135). But this is an Aunt Sally. Briefly, we can say about terms like 'physically strong', 'imaginative', 'quick-tempered' and so on that observable or dispositional behaviour may be essential for their verification, a criterion for their application, or (if we like) part of their meaning. But even this is doubtful and it is certainly not the whole story. A man *displays* (or perhaps does *not* display) his physical strength, quick temper, etc. *in* behaviour. But behaviour alone, at least in a fairly narrow sense of 'behaviour', is always insufficient and often ambiguous. We have to know something of its origins. We have to be assured, to take White's example, that Shakespeare and Newton *did* 'work out their masterpieces' by the appropriate power of their minds ('creativity'): that they did not do it under hypnosis, or dictation, or by accident, or by telepathic transmission from some other person. The mere product is not enough.

It is worth noting that White's picture derives from a particular (one is tempted to say, highly-specialized) concept of education, propounded by Peters, Hirst and others. According to this concept, 'the logically most fundamental objectives of all are those of a cognitive kind' (Hirst and Peters, 1970, p. 62); and this is cashed out elsewhere in the notion of 'worthwhile activities' and 'forms of knowledge' (for example, Peters, 1966, chapter V, Hirst and Peters, op. cit., pp. 60ff.). This concept has been criticized elsewhere (Downie, 1974); I raise the point here simply to show how restrictive it may be for creativity. Thus White asks (Dearden *et al.*, 1972, pp. 144ff.) how certain activities, thought by some teachers to encourage creativity, may be justified under 'the' concept of education. For instance, 'If the point of letting very young children play freely with paints, paper, clay, etc. is to familiarize them with (some of) the properties of these materials, then this is clearly a rational technique for starting children off on the road to producing aesthetically interesting pictures': it is a first move in the children being 'initiated into the domain of the aesthetic'. Apart from this, we are offered only two other types of justification:

'(a) they may be *therapeutically* valuable. Just as some disturbed adults find relief from their anxieties in dabbling in paint or scribbling down their thoughts, this may also be true for certain disturbed children;

(b) they may be worth making some provision for simply because, given that they are in no way immoral, children enjoy them.'

But, of course, we want none of these options. We want to say that there is some general power of the mind, 'creativity', which needs encouragement in children, and not just because we have to encourage it if they are to produce meritorious work, or because we want them to 'find relief from their anxieties', or to have a good time. We want to say that this power is a good thing in its own right, and should count as an educational good; that is, on my account (see chapter 1), something that can be directly gained by serious and sustained learning. In any case it seems clear that educational goods, however restrictively defined, may *overlap* with or be *coextensive* with other goods, for example, those that we might bring under the heading of 'mental health'

However, this does not take us far in any positive direction. We are in the fairly common position of needing to ask (as Toulmin, 1971, p. 38, well puts it) not 'What *do we mean* by it?', nor 'What *is* it?', but rather 'What *is there for one to mean* by it?' And the first point to be made, of course, is that there are all sorts of things that one might want to mean by it. Certainly there are all sorts of things that educationalists and others *do* mean, or think they mean, by 'creativity'. To map these out would be an immense task, particularly since very heterogeneous elements have gone to make up the use and popularity of the word (psychological research on 'divergent thinking', a dislike of unimaginative or 'authoritarian' teaching-methods, vague fantasies about 'self-expression', and so forth). Moreover, we should be trying to map a rapidly-changing territory; what different people have in mind when they talk of 'creativity' is in a state of flux. It will be some time (if ever – one possibility is that the word may pass out of use) before we can talk of 'the' concept of creativity, or even of two or three clearly-articulated concepts. (Elliott, 1971, outlines two general concepts in an interesting article.)

Making intelligent suggestions in such a situation requires some sort of intuition about the basic feelings that have promoted the notion; as, for instance, one might guess that 'autonomy' was promoted ultimately because of a thoroughly natural and understandable dislike of 'authority', 'indoctrination' and so forth. It does not (I hope) require immense intuition to conduct the same sort of exercise with creativity. The notion has become popular partly at least because of a reaction, or rather a set of reactions, against actual or imagined educational aims and methods. I will try to set these out in order.

First, there is the simple feeling that pupils may be (or may have been) subjected to too much mere information, rote learning, facts to be memorized, and so on. 'We want them to think and do things for themselves, not just be pumped full of facts.' So then one produces, or points to, situations in which pupils are demonstrably called on to think (in a strong sense of the word: perhaps we had better say 'to reason'): for instance, in which they have to solve equations or work out scientific problems. This may generate a second reaction: 'Yes, but all these situations have set and single solutions, "right answers". This seems to us still too restrictive – we want more than that.' So then – having taken time off to say that mathematics and science teachers are not only, or even chiefly, concerned to get 'right answers', but also with the reasoning and thought (perhaps even the 'creativity') of the pupils – one shows that there are fields in which 'right answers' is not an appropriate phrase. Artists, for instance, do not always 'solve problems' (though they often do (*pace* Elliott, ibid., p. 148): think of arranging the furniture of a room, making a church tower stand up, etc. It is dangerous to think of 'art' as consisting centrally of its most advanced cases, for example Shakespeare, Beethoven, Leonardo, etc.). Yet there can be better and worse art. Even chess-players talk of 'imaginative' or 'creative' moves, not always of 'the right' move. 'Is not all this enough to allow "creativity" to flourish as much as any sane person would want? Cannot pupils be "creative" *within* these activities?'

This is, I suppose, the orthodox line: neatly put by Peters's remark that 'creativity without competence is cant' (Dearden *et al.*, 1972, p. 519). 'Creative' is to mean something like 'imaginative'. Such an interpretation certainly seems comfortable enough, despite various difficulties about what might be meant by 'imaginative', and various temptations to reduce the notion of imagination to some kind of Rylean or adverbial status. At least we can be clear that we want to encourage and rate pupils for imaginativeness ('creativity') as well as, say, precision or sound working knowledge ('competence'); and we can admit that *some* school activities give no scope for imagination — even though it is not absolutely clear what sort of activities these are: perhaps at least they include rote-learning and various kinds of algorithmic performances. Will not this suffice for the advocates of creativity?

I feel quite certain that it would not suffice: and that we have at least to allow yet another reaction to be heard, which I think would go somewhat on these lines: 'That is still not good enough for us. You are still concerned too much with pupils being *good at* things, with "standards" if not with "right answers". Of course this is important, but it is not what we are talking about: and it is not the only thing we *can* talk about under the heading "education". What we are interested in is whether the pupils *do* things and *make* things in general or at all — not in whether they do and make things well or badly.' Can any sense be made of this?

Naturally it is easy to make nonsense of it. We could say 'Do you really want them to "do" or "make" just *anything*? After all, they can make "a mess", "trouble", "a scene", "mischief", etc. Surely you want them to do or make something *good*, or worthwhile?' But to this there are two possible lines of reply. One is to say 'Yes, all right, of course we will have a cut-off point in reference to which some kinds of doing or making will not count as "creative". But below that point what we value under this heading is *not* the merits of what is made, but rather the psychological state of the pupil trying to make it. We do not much care what the plasticine looks like at the end of the day — it's the fact that the pupil is "creating" that counts.' The other line is to say 'No, we prefer them to do *anything* rather than nothing: to be active rather than passive, or withdrawn, or inert, or sulking, or terrified — just as a psychotherapist often prefers disturbed children to act aggressively rather than remain locked up within themselves.'

I do not propose to defend the second line, because it is unnecessarily extravagant: except perhaps in certainly strictly limited contexts of a psychotherapeutic kind, one could not in fact let children do just *anything*. But it is worth mentioning, because it brings out an idea common to both lines: the idea that there is something *per se* valuable in 'doing' or 'making', and that this ought to be encouraged. The first line differs from the second, in effect, only by adding some such clause as 'other things being equal'. There is a close parallel, perhaps even something of an identity, here with certain interpretations of 'autonomy' which we noticed in the last chapter. Both share a picture which stresses the value of the person as an *agent*, and a feeling that it is in some general way better to do things for oneself than to be restricted by obedience to 'standards', 'right answers', or other people.

Various reasons combine to make this line, misty though it is, worth some pursuit. First, it seems to me at least tolerably clear that those who use the word 'creative' do not, in fact, mean 'imaginative'. Words like 'imaginative' and 'original' are indeed oriented towards public standards in something like the way that the orthodox literature stresses. Children and adults can and do engage in perhaps frenzied and sustained activity without ever producing anything which it would be even faintly plausible to call 'imaginative' or 'original': though we might call the people themselves 'productive' or 'fertile' or perhaps 'prolific'. Teachers, even under the lunacy-inducing pressures of new educational terminology, know quite well that most of what their pupils do is not imaginative or original. Some may be tempted to say 'Well, it's "original" in the sense that they originate it'; but of course that is not a sense of 'original' in modern English. Yet this temptation bears witness to the fact that they are trying to get behind the public-standards orientation of such words, and that is one reason why the neologism of 'creativity' has emerged.

Second, the line at least attempts some escape from the over-restrictive notion of education which I have mentioned earlier (see p. 113), according to which various 'powers of the mind' are treated wholly adverbially. The objection I want to raise here is the specific and simple one that, unless our picture allows us to consider such powers (however vague their title-words, like 'creativity', may be), we have no hope of getting clear about what they are or what sort of attention to bestow on them. Peters, for instance, is content to say 'The important point to stress, however, is that though these excellences are general qualities of mind they cannot be developed in a general sort of way' (ibid.). It is difficult even to understand this, since it is at least intelligible to suggest that certain very general features of a child's experience do in fact promote such qualities as imagination, determination, and so forth; and the (logical) fact, if it is a fact, that these qualities must be *displayed in* some specific activity or other is no argument to the contrary. In much the same way, fashionable courses in 'critical thinking' are not nonsense simply in the light of the point that one has to 'think critically' *within* some subject or discipline. For whatever power of the mind this term may mark, it marks some common psychological ground which might in principle be fertilized by some kind of training or educational experience. That we have as yet no clear understanding, let alone a taxonomy, of such powers of the mind merely points to the need for much harder work.

It would be possible to run the same sort of arguments with 'creativity' as we ran with 'autonomy'. We shall say, roughly, that though of course there are some (many) occasions when one should 'create' or 'be creative', there are also occasions when one should sit still, or absorb, or be passive, or whatever we can say that falls outside the concept of 'creativity' — just as there are some times when we should think and choose for ourselves ('autonomy') and other times when we should put ourselves in someone else's hands. 'Creativity', on this sort of interpretation, will be a virtue, a disposition governed by right reason, which functions when and only when it ought to — perhaps when writing or painting or playing with plasticine, but not when enjoying a well-earned rest or vaguely contemplating the scenery. To call someone 'uncreative' or 'lacking in creativity' will mean simply that he does not make or create when he ought to be doing so; and we can leave it fairly open when this 'ought' is to apply. There will, also, be a corresponding virtue, perhaps 'being reflective' or 'being able to sit back and absorb things', to cover the cases when one ought *not* to make and create: and a vice, 'over-activity' or 'compulsive creativity' or something of that kind, for those who do not possess this virtue.

But this, I think, would be to domesticate the notion too quickly. We might prefer to say that 'reflecting', 'absorbing', 'contemplating the scenery', etc., should not be contrasted with 'being creative', but rather treated as cases in which creativity is possible. There is, after all, a clear sense in which a man who revives his memories of a holiday abroad, or allows the beauty of a landscape to sink into his soul, or whatever, is making or creating something: even a day-dream or a fantasy could be made to count as a creation. Thus, instead of dividing human enterprises or modes of being into 'active' (where the virtue of 'creativity' is to operate) and 'passive' (where some other virtue is needed), we may want to say that people should be 'creative' in *all* enterprises and modes.

Can any sense be attached to this? One danger is to interpret 'creative' here along orthodox philosophical lines: 'All you are saying is that, whatever a person is engaged in — painting, reviving memories, contemplating scenery, etc. (and why leave out mathematics?) — he should do it *well*. This we agree with, but it was precisely the move you rejected earlier. If you are not saying that, then you can only be saying that human beings *do*, in fact, engage in these various activities: that in so far as they are human (rather than stones or bits of wood) they "do" and "make" things all the time: that they just *are* "creative". If you are not interested in their doing things well, and if *anything* they engage in counts as "creating", what can you mean by saying you want to *encourage* "creativity"?'

To answer this we must go back to the question of what a person is allowed to 'do' or 'make' if we are to allow ourselves to speak of his being 'creative'. We thought of disallowing 'a mess', 'trouble', etc. But we can disallow these on two quite different criteria. One criterion is simply that what is created is not worthwhile (or 'original', or 'imaginative', or whatever standards we wish to apply drawn from the public world). The other criterion is more difficult to state; but it has something to do with the notion of making some sort of attempt on the world, by way of understanding it or changing it or adding to it, which is meaningful to the person making the attempt in that it is connected with his own desires. Of course this is hopelessly vague; but we can see, for instance, that a painting or scrawl which was 'a mess' would not count as creative if produced by the accidental upsetting of ink-wells, but might count as such if deliberately produced by (say) a young child or a psychotic patient 'to express himself'. By public standards it is 'a mess' (and of course it *is* 'a mess', because the term is governed by those standards); but by the standards of creativity – that is, by *other* public standards which relate to the person's psychology rather than to the art critic's norms – it may be symptomatic of something desirable having happened.

'Self-expression' is not a good word to express this desirability, however. In a sense one may 'express oneself' by screaming, weeping, and other semi-voluntary behaviour. Nor is 'active' (as against 'passive') of much help; the male is not more 'creative' in the sexual act simply because he is, in one obvious sense, more 'active' – the ability to *respond to* the world is as important as the ability to *operate on* it. To use this (I hope inoffensive and perhaps paradigmatic) example, if we were to ask what made sexual behaviour 'creative' (not procreative), our answer would have something to do with the degree of consciousness used, and significance invested, in it by a person. We should at least *not* be saying that 'creative' means 'conforming to the highest standards of the *techne* of love-making', or that it meant 'active' in the sense of 'energetic'. We should, rather, be trying to distinguish the non-conscious coming together of animals from the conscious and significant enterprise of persons.

It is difficult to describe this criterion without imposing too narrow a moral vision on it. Thus it is fatally easy to impose some kind of protestant-ethic view, as if in commending creativity we had to single out for commendation such things as hard work, concentration, diligence, earnestness, etc. (as against play, pleasure, humour and so forth), or to impose a sentimental notion of 'love', 'affection' and 'unselfishness' (as against the aggressive bite which is very evident in most 'creations' at a high level). Clinical psychologists might talk here, I think, of 'ego-strength', and contemporary philosophers of 'rationality' or 'language-using'. Neither of these are really satisfactory, because we are talking of something which in a way lies behind both: the potential that conscious creatures have for dealing with the world.

This potential is, of course, to some degree actual for anyone we should want to call human or conscious; and equally, even the most 'creative' person falls short of being 'creative' all the time – for instance, he goes to sleep. The opposite of 'creative', on our account, is something like 'unconscious': and the borderline cases will be cases of a person having such a narrow world to respond to or operate on that we have doubts about calling it 'a world' at all – for instance, a man being half-asleep and dreaming, or a psychotic person whose world consists almost entirely of the narrow circle of his own fantasies. 'Conscious', though attributable absolutely (either a conscious being or not), may also be used to admit of degrees: degrees which vary from person to person and time to time. In this sense, consciousness can be equated with creativity: creativity is the operation of consciousness on the world.

All this may sound not only vague but grotesquely high-falutin' (Elliott, 1971, pp. 151–2, offers one or two interesting descriptions); but it is, I think, what lies at the back of the minds of many practising teachers. Many pupils (and many adults, come to that) appear, to those that know them well, as only semi-conscious or half-alive. It is not that they are all inert; on the contrary, quite a few of them are senselessly aggressive. It is not that they all fail to meet the requirements of the academic disciplines; on the contrary, a pupil who is obsessed and limited by mathematical computations may be among the least 'creative' (think of an *idiot savant*). It is rather that – at school, at least, though perhaps not in the gang or on the football field – their general consciousness and operant desires are at a low ebb. They are only half *there*, and it is quite possible to feel that they might as well not be there at all.

On this interpretation, 'creativity' marks not so much *a* 'power of the mind' as *the* 'power of the mind'. Perhaps after all 'ego-strength' is not too disastrous a translation: it is certainly less misleading than such terms as 'intelligent', 'well-educated', 'critical', 'serious' and other such candidates. The notion has something in common with what Mary Warnock seems to want to make 'imagination' mean: 'It is what enables one to see things as *significant*' (Peters, 1973, p. 112). But there is an enormous amount of work to do here, by way of offering much more detailed and compelling descriptions: what I have said above may do no more than point to the need for bridging the gap between the nebulous feelings that teachers and others have on the one hand, and a clear and full philosophical or phenomenological account on the other.

It now needs to be very firmly declared that many of the practical moves commonly associated with 'creativity' in education are, to say the least, questionable. Certainly no 'conclusions' can be drawn from the notion as I have interpreted it. For instance, it is not clear that 'creativity' has been diminished or repressed by 'authoritarian' teaching-methods (whatever this might mean), or by a lot of rote-learning or information-giving. It is not clear that 'looser' or less structured activities, in which there are no 'right answers' and the notion of 'standards' is more fluid, encourage creativity; quite possibly it is encouraged more by giving children experience of success in tightly-structured, clear-cut forms of learning. It is not clear that 'strong discipline', or 'extrinsic motivation', or any of the things commonly under fire from those who propound creativity, are in fact a hindrance to it. Finally, it is not clear whether the improvement of creativity is something which can be effectively undertaken in the *classroom* at all; my own guess would be that we need quite a different sort of 'social base' to develop such things, of a kind more like that which I have elsewhere described (Wilson, 1972b, part 4). Teachers and others concerned with creativity — if I have interpreted their concern aright in my account of it — must start from scratch. Almost nothing is *known* about how to develop creativity, and it is better to think for oneself, in relation to the children one can actually affect, rather than be distracted by the irrelevance of most 'experimental' psychology (Harré, 1974). There are, obviously, things which any sensible person can start to think about here; for instance, the importance of language to consciousness, the importance of love and personal attention as a background, the importance of encouraging and rewarding a child's conscious attempts on the world, and so forth. What we require here is the determined advancement of common sense, aided by anything that philosophers or psychotherapists have to tell us; and practically everything remains to be done.

I want to conclude by looking at one or two methodological points, arising from 'creativity', 'autonomy' and other similar notions. I have argued, if only by implication, that there *is* need of a term to mark an important concept in this area; and I have treated 'creativity' as such a term. I am not at all sure that it is the best possible candidate; certainly it suggests something rather inflated, and certainly it has distracted its users and critics down all sorts of useless alleys. But it seems *a* possible candidate, unlike 'autonomy', which seems to me at least to mark nothing both clear and important, certainly in the interpretations normally put forward.

But do we need a candidate at all? At the end of the last chapter I advanced the Austinian claim that 'ordinary language' was likely to contain all or most of what we needed for our purposes; will not this do for 'creativity' as well as 'autonomy' and all the other terms of art that have come into prominence over the last few decades? About 'creativity' we could say: 'We know already that we want children to make conscious attempts on the world, to develop "ego-strength" and "rationality": nothing is gained by inventing a new word. You have already described, in down-to-earth language, how some pupils appear "semi-conscious" or "only half there"; fuller and more accurate descriptions can only come from the same sort of language.'

But, as the metaphorical and semi-technical terms in this account themselves show, we do need a word. It is not entirely true that 'we know already'; in trying to elucidate the concept for which we want 'creativity' to stand, we are not so much recovering knowledge that we have somewhere at the back of our minds, as assembling various features of our experience which we wish to put together for a certain (new) purpose: much as one might need a word, 'democracy', *before* the actual existence of democracies in political practice, and even though all the particular features of 'democracy' were individually known to us. What seems to have happened is that — for good or bad reasons — certain very general aspects of the human mind have vaguely filtered into the consciousness of educators in recent years, and need to be clarified and identified by a new terminology.

It is, I think, unsurprising that the nearest existing terminology — 'ego-strength' is not the only example — is to be found in the language of psychotherapy. The general approach initiated by Freud antedated 'progressive' education by some little time, and had already established technical terms of its own. Unfortunately, it was both too redolent of a mechanistic or hydrodynamic model and too specialized to gain currency in the wider context of education. Apart from philosophy, post-Freudian psychology is the most obvious example of a sustained and non-dogmatic approach to the 'powers of the mind' in which educators are interested (other candidates would include various religious descriptions, and some Piagetian research). Now that educators are more conscious of this interest, it is not to be wondered at if they are retreading something of the same ground.

The position at present is that there is an *embarras de richesse* of nebulous terms, *all* of which may perhaps testify to the current interest in the *same* aspects of the human mind. Thus Elliott (1971, p. 150):

> We should not suppose that because our present concept of creativity collects together a number of highly important matters it must be pretentious or inflated. It is simply a focus of human hopes and aspirations. In reflecting upon it we relate the ideas of freedom, founding, innovation, progress and autonomy to education . . .

and so on: he might as well have thrown in 'critical thinking' for good measure. It would be possible to advance an argument, I suppose, which named 'autonomy' as the candidate for the concept which I have interpreted under 'creativity'; and maybe there are other candidates among the current jargon.

All this is rather depressing, and I do not think progress towards a clear and agreed set of terms and concepts will be swift. But, for the reasons I have given, it would be wrong to abandon them altogether. We can only hope that future educators will have the benefit of enough man-hours of philosophizing about them to establish linguistic conventions within which we can work. On the credit side, however, it does seem that the interest which causes the confusion is a genuine one; that is, educators do need to think long and hard not only in terms of the prevailing philosophical orthodoxy, whose 'most fundamental objectives of all are those of a cognitive kind' (Hirst and Peters, 1970, p. 62), but also in terms of 'general powers of the mind' and of human consciousness in general. However dangerous and rambling these paths, it may be wise not to let go of 'creativity' until we have mapped at least the most important of them.

Postscript

I hinted in the introduction that, if this book is successful at all, it should succeed in two quite different ways. Now that we have reached the end of it, we may usefully elaborate each of these ways briefly and thus consolidate them.

1 First there is the question of what 'thesis' or 'substantive opinions': I have tried to advance. Now perhaps all philosophers can do (and it is a lot) is to connect various concepts with each other; to show in what ways we can, and in what we cannot, argue and act with consistency and reason. However, it seems to me that there are certain very obvious *facts* about our own schools (and those of a great many other societies) which, taken in conjunction with these conceptual points, do strongly suggest some practical conclusions, about which action ought to be taken. I speak here, of course, not as a philosopher but (if with any authority at all) as an ex-teacher and somebody in reasonably close contact with the educational system; and in any case the reader must judge the facts for himself. But they seem sufficiently obvious to be worth connecting, albeit briefly, with our conceptual findings.

(a) To begin with, I suspect that many people are not sufficiently concerned with *education* at all: that is, as we saw in chapter 1, with serious and sustained *learning*. Teachers, for the most part, still are so concerned; but the interests of politicians, governments, local authorities, unions and even parents seem to be rather different. They have their eyes on other than educational goods: on some kind of social theory or ideology, on the job market, on financial and economic matters, on wages and salaries, on social status, on passing examinations that will get pupils better jobs, and so on. None of these is *necessarily* connected with sustained and serious learning as such: there are, no doubt, contingent connections, but it is not clear just how strong they are. The same applies to a very large proportion of so-called 'educational research': sociologists, economists and others have interests

123

often far removed from learning, and more to do with the social or economic system than with education. A crucial question for teachers here is how much of the time in school, for particular sorts of pupils, needs to be spent on learning as against other activities; and what practical arrangements should be made to cater for the distinction between the two.

(b) Second, and perhaps because of this, there seems to be a remarkable failure to *trust* anyone with the job of educating people, or even to realize the conditions necessary for the job to be done at all. In chapter 2 we outlined the necessity for a 'potent' and 'autonomous' school, in which a good deal more power would have to be given to teachers than is now the case. Most schools, both in the UK and elsewhere, are not like this at all. This lack of trust extends so far that — as many teachers know very well from personal experience — the proper use of discipline and authority (chapters 3 and 4) has, in many schools, simply disappeared. Not only do teachers not have enough power to educate, some of them barely have enough power to survive. Many different kinds of chaos, both in schools and society, are obviously connected with this; and it presents a very sharp contrast with those schools, past and present (now, in the UK, mostly the independent schools), where education is taken seriously and the teachers are trusted with power.

(c) This failure to trust, a fairly general feature of our own and other similar societies, can only be remedied by a firm conceptual grasp of the principles relevant to authority, and by contractual negotiation: these we outlined in chapter 4. The educational situation reflects only one instance of our failure: we have to see through the *general* fantasies that we can do without authority, sanctions and other inexpellable notions altogether, and that hanging on to, or trying to revive, some 'moral authority', 'general consensus', 'traditional respect', or whatever, will provide a solution. We have above all to negotiate *clear* and *properly-enforced* contracts. When we have succeeded in doing this, we shall (perhaps for the first time) be able to get on with the job of educating, without constant political and social distraction.

Turning to the much more complicated question of the content of education, we can at least claim to have taken a few steps forward:

(d) We have reminded ourselves, in chapter 5, of the fairly stringent requirements of anything properly to be called a *curriculum*, in particular the requirement that the learning be structured. The sophistication of these requirements reminds us — for I think the fact is obvious — that substantial numbers of children are not 'suited' (as we put it) for very much of this sort of learning. In so far as our schools — and this too I take to be a fact — at least pretend, by keeping our children till the age of 16 within a framework of classroom-periods, to be engaging them in curricular studies, they are doing the wrong sort of job. Not only shall we fail to teach them much at this sophisticated level, but also — because of our pretence — we shall fail to teach them those important things which are, in fact, suitable: amongst these we might count literacy, basic moral education, and various practical competencies which will be of direct use to them and to society in general.

(e) From our consideration of 'subjects' (chapter 6) it appears that, until we have a more effective taxonomic system than we now possess, we shall do best to rely on existing reference-groups (at universities and elsewhere) as a criterion of demarcation. That is, for the serious pursuit of subjects for their own sake, we need to look at what serious people who are not under social or other pressures consider as worthwhile subjects of study in themselves. The most important task in this context is getting our pupils to be serious about, or to love, *some* 'subject' or type of study for its own sake; and for this the existence of such traditions and reference-groups is extremely important. We have ourselves a great deal to learn about what is attractive, to what sorts of people, in these serious studies; but we shall only make progress if we keep the studies intact, rather than dismantling them in the supposed interests of 'relevance' or 'what interests the pupils'.

(f) Finally, in considering a pair of supposed virtues or mental powers ('autonomy' in chapter 7 and 'creativity' in chapter 8), we saw the importance of avoiding any too-rapid or partisan attachment to specific 'values' or 'ideologies'. In some cases, like 'autonomy', we know quite well (when we keep our heads) what we want already, and do not need a new slogan. In others, as perhaps with 'creativity', it may be that we are fighting our way towards a new awareness of what is of basic importance to the human mind; the importance of the self's general powers to deal with the outside world. These general powers of the mind badly need to be mapped more precisely, but inasmuch as it is possible that they may be acquired by learning, they represent genuine educational objectives. However, it is more than likely that the *classroom* is not the best area in which to develop and encourage such powers; we need to take other aspects of school life much more seriously.

Even these tentative steps, I think, have pretty obvious practical bearings. We can be clear that curricular or 'academic' learning is only part of a school's job. But it is an important part; and it is disastrous to try to cater for other, more 'progressive', sets of objectives by dismantling this set. We need to keep that intact and, inevitably, firmly based on

125

'traditional' lines. Then we have somehow to devise quite *other* methods for the quite *different* content that may be marked by the titles of virtues or powers of the mind. In other words, any serious school must retain, rather than water down, the curricular learning of traditional subjects and disciplines, together with whatever other classroom-learning may be suitable for its pupils: and also deal with the general area which we might label 'socialization', 'moral education', 'mental health', 'character-building' or whatever by contexts and types of experience which will mostly be *outside* the classroom (see Wilson, 1972b, part 4).

These conclusions seem to me wholly obvious. More importantly, they would (I think) have seemed obvious to most educators until comparatively recently. For they were clear that *both* these two tasks were necessary for education; indeed, they would usually have given priority to the latter. The fact, if it is a fact, that their theories and practices were often based on particular ideals, which we might now wish to challenge, is not here relevant; it does not follow from this that we should do nothing, for fear of getting our hands dirty. Yet, to pass an admittedly over-generalized judgment, it seems to me that in a great many schools neither task is taken seriously. Certainly, both tasks are constantly discussed, there are continual conferences, working-parties and so on about 'the curriculum', 'pastoral care', 'moral education', and other such. But I venture to say that most of such discussions are not only extremely intellectually confused, but also largely disconnected from the practical action which even common sense (let alone philosophy) would dictate. To repeat a point made in chapter 2, we *know* that children ought to be made to read, write and count; that they should not be allowed to get away with vandalism, bullying, stealing, insolence, and many other things. But, because we are nervous about entrusting and exercising power, we conduct endless discussions rather than acting.

It is important, however, that we act in full knowledge. Common sense may itself easily become partisan, or turn into another 'ideology' (labelled, I suppose, in this case something like 'traditionalist', 'authoritarian', or whatever). We need to be clear not only that certain things must be done, but also why they must be. It is not until enough people in the business properly understand the 'why' that we can proceed on a secure and rationally-agreed basis, rather than remaining subject to the swinging pendulum of fashion. I have tried to show in this book that certain things are required for education. That means, first, that they are required for *education*, and not for the benefit of some ideology; and second, that they are *required*, that they are necessities and not just pious hopes.

2 These, then, are roughly the 'substantive' or 'practical' conclusions to which our discussion seems to point. To many people they may not seem 'practical' enough. Even if this were the sort of book for

advancing a more detailed schedule for practical action, however, I should have some doubts about how much would actually be gained by doing this. For it is, I think, a point of logic — not just a tolerably sound empirical generalization — that in this sort of business almost everything turns on the individual coming to see the reasons for himself. When he has seen them and (to put it dramatically) been inspired by their force, then it is likely to be he himself, not the educational philosopher, who can best judge in detail about what needs to be done. If, on the other hand, he does not see them for himself, then no amount of bullying or propaganda will improve matters; for it is not a matter of persuading teachers and others to buy a particular package, a set of 'conclusions' or 'recommendations' in a glossy cover, but a matter of getting them to think straight.

That is why my chief hope is that this book, as much by its style as by its content or 'conclusions', will encourage teachers and others to undertake the general task of clear conceptual thinking for themselves. It is, ultimately, their responsibility. In what is perhaps the most influential book about education written in the last few decades, Professor Peters says that 'this book is only written for those who take seriously the question "What ought I to do?" '; and the importance of this notion of seriousness for what he says later in the book is entirely clear (Peters, 1966, p. 116. Cf. pp. 124–5, 162–3 and elsewhere). Yet it is also clear that we are not always as serious as we should be. We defend ourselves against seriousness by all sorts of methods, of which (at least amongst academics and educators) a kind of deliberate earnestness and deference to pseudo-scholarship is one of the most common. We have somehow both to avoid this, and to avoid running wild.

One of the best models for seriousness is the Socratic dialogues. Amongst the features that seem to me of especial relevance are: first, that they are *dialogues* and not monologues; second, that they combine intense truth-seeking with a relaxed and often humorous style; and third, that they do not always issue in 'conclusions'. They represent rather a form of life into which any self-respecting person needs — to borrow yet again from Peters — to be 'initiated' and to get himself 'on the inside' of (ibid., chapter 2). Conditions of communication in most of our institutions, as well as our own psychological failings, make such a model hard to realize in practice. But we have to do our best.

It is, I think, only when we can do this effectively that we can even begin to see how much help we can get from psychologists, sociologists, and other 'experts' who write about education. The reader will have observed that I have often referred to their work in a somewhat brusque and dismissive way. What anybody says has, of course, some *prima facie* right to be taken seriously, and I do not want to leave the reader with the impression that they have nothing to contribute. Just what they actually do contribute to *education*, however, would require very careful and detailed examination. My own view, some illustrations of which I have given elsewhere (Wilson, 1972a), is that most of the empirical disciplines as now institutionalized — I mean, what now goes on under the headings of 'psychology (sociology, etc.) of education', 'educational theory', 'curriculum studies', etc. — do not, in fact, contribute very much. There are various reasons for this which I here pass over (Wilson, 1975, chapters 2 and 3 covers some of this ground); and there are, of course, honourable exceptions. Moreover, some philosophers at least — to judge from their writings — take a much less severe view than I do. But the point remains that ordinary teachers and educators must not *take it for granted* that what these 'experts' say is right, or even that it is coherent. Such matters have to be fought out, dialectically and in detail; and the chief need of most teachers, as I see it, is enough nerve and a clear enough head to fight properly.

Most of us — that is, when we are not wholly occupied in trying to survive in a difficult and chaotic world — have strong feelings about education: what we do not have is intellectual clarity. Indeed, there are times when one almost comes to think that any attempt at clarity will be bitterly resisted, because it seems too threatening. There is, certainly, a contemporary dislike of 'cold logic', 'intellectualizing', 'analysis', even 'rationality': it is as if the whole business of *making distinctions* — of splitting things up and trying to deal with them separately — alarmed many people. Perhaps the idea of identifying differences itself seems unfriendly or 'undemocratic', and goes against the feeling of warm and fraternal solidarity marked by such terms as 'integration' and 'consensus'. Many men are frightened even by tough-minded argument, as if arguing meant quarrelling. We need to learn how to argue, and to welcome argument, before we can make much progress.

References

Bambrough, R. (1956), 'Plato's Political Analogies', in *Philosophy, Politics and Society*, 1st series, ed. P. Laslett, Blackwell.
Barrow, R. (1974), 'Who are the Philosopher-kings?', in *Proceedings of the Philosophy of Education Society of Great Britain*, Supplementary Issue, vol. VIII, no. 2, Blackwell.
Barrow, R. (1975), *Plato, Utilitarianism and Education*, Routledge & Kegan Paul.
Bloom, B. *et al.* (1964), *Taxonomy of Educational Objectives*, David McKay.
Dearden, R. F. (1968), *Philosophy of Primary Education*, Routledge & Kegan Paul.
Dearden, R. F., Hirst, P. H. and Peters, R. S. (eds) (1972), *Education and the Development of Reason*, Routledge & Kegan Paul.
Downie, R. S. *et al.* (1974), *Education and Personal Relationships*, Methuen.
Elliott, R. (1971), 'Versions of Creativity', in *Proceedings of the Philosophy of Education Society of Great Britain*, Supplementary Volume, vol. V, no. 2, Blackwell.
Hare, R. M. (1963), *Freedom and Reason*, Oxford University Press.
Harré, R. (1974), 'Some Remarks on "Rule" as a Scientific Concept', in *Understanding Other Persons*, ed. T. Mischel, Blackwell.
Harré, R. and Secord, P. F. (1972), *The Explanation of Social Behaviour*, Blackwell.
Hart, H. L. A. (1963), *Law, Liberty and Morality*, Oxford University Press.
Hirst, P. H. (1974), *Knowledge and the Curriculum*, Routledge & Kegan Paul.
Hirst, P. H. and Peters, R. S. (1970), *The Logic of Education*, Routledge & Kegan Paul.
Honderich, T. (1969), *Punishment*, Hutchinson.
Johnson, H. T. (1968), *Foundations of Curriculum*, Merrill, Columbus, Ohio.
Lucas, C. J. (ed.) (1969), *What is Philosophy of Education?*, Collier Macmillan.

References

Lucas, J. R. (1966), *Principles of Politics*, Oxford University Press.
McPhail, P. *et al.* (1972), *Moral Education in the Secondary School*, Longmans.
Martin, J. (ed.) (1970), *Readings in the Philosophy of Education: A Study of Curriculum*, Allyn & Bacon, Boston.
O'Connor, D. J. (1957), *An Introduction to the Philosophy of Education*, Routledge & Kegan Paul.
Peters, R. S. (1966), *Ethics and Education*, Allen & Unwin.
Peters, R. S. (ed.) (1973), *The Philosophy of Education*, Oxford Readings, Oxford University Press.
Peters, R. S. (1974), *Psychology and Ethical Development*, Allen & Unwin.
Pitkin, H. (1972), 'Obligation and Consent', in *Philosophy, Politics and Society*, 4th series, ed. P. Laslett *et al.*, Blackwell.
Popper, K. R. (1966), *The Open Society and its Enemies*, Routledge & Kegan Paul.
Quinton, A. (1973), *The Nature of Things*, Routledge & Kegan Paul.
Rawls, J. (1972), *A Theory of Justice*, Oxford University Press.
Richmond, W. K. (1971), *The School Curriculum*, Methuen.
Rugg, H. (1936), *American Life and the School Curriculum*, Ginn.
Ryan, A. (ed.) (1973), *The Philosophy of Social Explanation*, Oxford University Press.
Saunders, T. J. (1970), translation of Plato's *Laws*, Penguin Books.
Sinclair, T. A. (1962), translation of Aristotle's *Politics*, Penguin Books.
Strawson, P. F. (1962), *Freedom and Resentment*, Oxford University Press.
Taba, H. (1962), *Curriculum Development*, Harcourt, Brace & World.
Thomson, J. A. K. (1955), translation of Aristotle's *Nicomachean Ethics*, Penguin Books.
Tibble, J. W. (ed.) (1966), *The Study of Education*, Routledge & Kegan Paul.
Toulmin, S. (1971), 'The Concept of "Stages" in Psychological Development', in *Cognitive Development and Epistemology*, ed. T. Mischel, Academic Press, New York.
White, J. P. (1973), *Towards a Compulsory Curriculum*, Routledge & Kegan Paul.
Wilson, J. (1971), *Education in Religion and the Emotions*, Heinemann.
Wilson, J. (1972a), *Philosophy and Educational Research*, NFER, Slough.
Wilson, J. (1972b), *Practical Methods of Moral Education*, Heinemann.
Wilson, J. (1973), *The Assessment of Morality*, NFER, Slough.
Wilson, J. (1975), *Educational Theory and the Preparation of Teachers*, NFER, Slough.
Wilson, P. S. (1971), *Interest and Discipline in Education*, Routledge & Kegan Paul.
Winch, P. (1959–60), 'Nature and Convention', in *Proceedings of the Aristotelian Society*.
Yudkin, M. (1969), *General Education*, Penguin Books.

Students Library of Education

General Editor   Lionel Elvin

From College to Classroom: The Probationary Year. Derek Hanson and Margaret Herrington. 128 pp.

The Study of Education. J. W. Tibble. 240 pp.

METHOD

Change in Art Education. Dick Field. 132 pp.

Changing Aims in Religious Education. Edwin Cox. 108 pp.

Children and Learning to Read. Elizabeth J. Goodacre. 128 pp.

Discovery Learning in the Primary School. John Foster. 158 pp.

Environmental Studies. D. G. Watts. 128 pp.

*The Future of the Sixth Form.** A. D. C. Peterson. 96 pp.

*Inspecting and the Inspectorate.** John Blackie. 112 pp.

*The Learning of History.** D. G. Watts. 128 pp.

*The Middle School Experiment.** Reese Edwards. 112 pp.

Reading in Primary Schools. Geoffrey R. Roberts. 108 pp.

Spelling: Caught or Taught? Margaret L. Peters. 96 pp.

Students into Teachers: Experiences of Probationers in Schools. Mildred Collins. 112 pp.

HISTORY

*Advisory Councils and Committees in Education.** Maurice Kogan and Tim Packwood. 136 pp.

The American Influence on English Education. W. H. G. Armytage. 128 pp.

The Changing Sixth Form in the Twentieth Century. A. D. Edwards. 115 pp.

*Church, State and Schools in Britain 1800–1970.** James Murphy. 192 pp.

*English Education and the Radicals 1780–1850.** Harold Silver. 148 pp.

*English Primary Education and the Progressives 1914–1939.** R. J. W. Selleck. 206 pp.

The Evolution of the Comprehensive School 1926–1972. David Rubinstein and Brian Simon. 148 pp.

The Evolution of the Nursery-Infant School. Nanette Whitbread. 160 pp.

The Foundations of Twentieth-Century Education. E. Eaglesham. 128 pp.

The French Influence on English Education. W. H. G. Armytage. 128 pp.

*The German Influence on English Education. W. H. G. Armytage. 142 pp.

Mediaeval Education and the Reformation. J. Lawson. 128 pp.

Recent Education from Local Sources. Malcolm Seaborne. 128 pp.

*The Russian Influence on English Education. W. H. G. Armytage. 138 pp.

Secondary School Reorganization in England and Wales. Alun Griffiths. 128 pp.

Social Change and the Schools: 1918–1944. Gerald Bernbaum. 128 pp.

The Social Origins of English Education. Joan Simon. 132 pp.

PHILOSOPHY

Education and the Concept of Mental Health. John Wilson. 99 pp.

Indoctrination and Education. I. A. Snook. 128 pp.

Interest and Discipline in Education. P. S. Wilson. 142 pp.

The Logic of Education. P. H. Hirst and R. S. Peters. 196 pp.

Philosophy and the Teacher. Edited by D. I. Lloyd. 180 pp.

The Philosophy of Primary Education. R. F. Dearden. 208 pp.

Plato and Education. Robin Barrow. 96 pp.

Problems in Primary Education. R. F. Dearden. 160 pp.

PSYCHOLOGY

Creativity and Education. Hugh Lytton. 144 pp.

Group Study for Teachers. Elizabeth Richardson. 144 pp.

Human Learning: A Developmental Analysis. H. S. N. McFarland. 136 pp.

An Introduction to Educational Measurement. D. Pidgeon and A. Yates. 122 pp.

Modern Educational Psychology: An Historical Introduction. E. G. S. Evans. 118 pp.

An Outline of Piaget's Developmental Psychology. Ruth M. Beard. 144 pp.

Personality, Learning and Teaching. George D. Handley. 126 pp.

*Teacher Expectations and Pupil Learning. Roy Nash. 128 pp.

Teacher and Pupil: Some Socio-Psychological Aspects. Philip Gammage. 128 pp.

Troublesome Children in Class. Irene E. Caspari. 160 pp.

SOCIOLOGY

Basic Readings in the Sociology of Education. D. F. Swift. 368 pp.
Class, Culture and the Curriculum. Denis Lawton. 140 pp.
Culture, Industrialisation and Education. G. H. Bantock. 108 pp.
*Education at Home and Abroad. Joseph Lauwerys and Graham Tayar. 144 pp.
Education, Work and Leisure. Harold Entwistle. 118 pp.
The Organization of Schooling: A Study of Educational Grouping Practices. Alfred Yates. 116 pp.
*Political Education in a Democracy. Harold Entwistle. 144 pp.
The Role of the Pupil. Barbara Calvert. 160 pp.
The Role of the Teacher. Eric Hoyle. 112 pp.
The Social Context of the School. S. John Eggleston. 128 pp.
The Sociology of Educational Ideas. Julia Evetts. 176 pp.

CURRICULUM STUDIES

*Towards a Compulsory Curriculum. J. P. White. 122 pp.

INTERDISCIPLINARY STUDIES

*Educational Theory: An Introduction. T. W. Moore. 116 pp.
Perspectives on Plowden. R. S. Peters. 116 pp.
*The Role of the Head. Edited by R. S. Peters. 136 pp.

* Library edition only